Living in the Five-Sense World

Kevin W. McPeek, Sr.

Bloomington, IN   Milton Keynes, UK
authorHOUSE®

AuthorHouse™
1663 Liberty Drive, Suite 200
Bloomington, IN 47403
www.authorhouse.com
Phone: 1-800-839-8640

AuthorHouse™ *UK Ltd.*
500 Avebury Boulevard
Central Milton Keynes, MK9 2BE
www.authorhouse.co.uk
Phone: 08001974150

© 2007 Kevin W. McPeek, Sr.. All rights reserved.

No part of this book may be reproduced, stored in a retrieval system, or transmitted by any means without the written permission of the author.

First published by AuthorHouse   4/23/2007

ISBN: 978-1-4343-0927-3 (e)
ISBN: 978-1-4343-0926-6 (sc)
ISBN: 978-1-4343-0925-9 (hc)

Library of Congress Control Number: 2007902749

Printed in the United States of America
Bloomington, Indiana

This book is printed on acid-free paper.

Introduction

In the first book of Moses, referred to in the King James Bible as Genesis, Moses writes in chapter one, verse one, "In the beginning God created the heaven and the earth." Also in chapter one, verse thirty-one, Moses writes, "And God saw everything he had made, and, behold, it was very good. And the evening and the morning were the sixth day." On the seventh day God rested.

Whether one believes Moses' story of creation or the theory of evolution, perhaps the reader will agree on the following ideas. Moses was speaking metaphorically. We don't know how long a day is in God's world. And we know the Earth is billions of years old. The writer subscribes to all three possibilities. With that in mind, hopefully we can all agree that according to Moses, God had created everything in the material world in six days. Sometime after the seventh day, God created Adam and Eve; Adam, from the dust of the earth and Eve from Adam's rib.

Although God had provided Adam and Eve with limited, finite minds, he did provide them with physical bodies that would last for hundreds of human years on planet Earth. Adam would die 930 years later.

God also gave Adam and Eve emotional and spiritual bodies. He knew that if Adam and Eve would achieve balance within their four bodies, they would be forever happy in this environment.

God felt so good about his creation of man and woman that he also gave them the mental capabilities to make decisions on their own. They had God's complete trust, so he gave them dominion over the entire world he had created just for them.

We human beings refer to the Garden of Eden as a paradise—a utopia, a perfect blend of the five human senses. According to Moses, Adam and Eve had been forbidden by God to eat the fruit of the tree of knowledge (located within the garden), but it did not take long for an insider to influence their better judgment. After consuming the fruit cocktail, their emotional bodies suddenly exploded and their ego/personalities expanded. This made them feel separated from God and each other.

The cosmos shuddered because it realized that every human being in generations to come would feel separated from God and each other because of their expanded egos.

The good versus-bad concept was now forged in steel and aligned with punishment and judgment. The truth would be forgotten, veiled in secrecy for many generations to come. Man's confusion would keep him isolated, separated, and desperate to know his true purpose.

But in a dimension near by, a very wise old soul named Nebulon had been observing God's creation of the Milky Way galaxy since its inception. Now that it was nearing completion, Nebulon's love for this creation was expanding. God noticed this and asked, "Are you are fond of my creation Nebulon?"

Nebulon replied, "I am, but why have you spent so much of your time and energy creating a galaxy that appears so lifeless and colorless when compared to all your other creations? Even the planet you refer to as Earth, with all its living organisms, is dull and drab! It appears to me that you will have to constantly create abundance because this physical creation cannot sustain itself."

God smiled on Nebulon, stating, "You have always been a very wise and trusted companion of mine. It does not surprise me in the least to hear how you feel about my newest creation. It is very different from all the others, but it will be very special when I am finally finished."

Nebulon smiled back at God, appreciating his wisdom, unconditional love, and acknowledgment.

God felt Nebulon's thoughts while he continued his vibrant explanation. "The reason the Milky Way galaxy is so lifeless and colorless and planet Earth appears dull and drab is because the life forms that I have created cannot survive my full essence. So I will have to continually create abundance to sustain the existence of the Milky Way galaxy. But I want you to know I do this for you and all the other spiritual beings I have created in my image. I wanted to give you and the others an opportunity to experience human life on planet Earth!"

Nebulon asked, "Why would I want to give up my eternal existence with you in order to take on the life of a limited human being, on a planet that is so dull and drab?"

God patiently began to explain, "As a spiritual being, you embrace your essence. Your divinity presents a beautiful picture of our relationship within the cosmos. And although you can see with your divine eye my creation of the Milky Way galaxy, I know you can only feel universal love for the common good."

Nebulon's field of vibrating energy was a dead giveaway. "Of course that is what I am feeling, Lord. That is my divine purpose."

God continued, "I created you as a one-dimensional vibrating source of energy, which is capable of moving through and around all the dimensions in all my creations. But when you are born again as a physical human being, you will have a three-dimensional body that is limited to living in just one four-dimensional world, the Milky Way galaxy. You will have an intellectual body, a physical body, an emotional body, and your current spiritual body."

Nebulon responded, "That's a lot of bodies, Lord!"

God was now laughing. "I guess I should explain the process for becoming a human being on planet Earth. Taking on a physical body doesn't mean your spiritual body dies. I have arranged for your spiritual body to be permeated in every human cell. As the human cells of the physical body die, the spiritual body will constrict itself, until new human cells are generated. The spirit will always maintain its integrity and vibration level. You and I will always be connected just as we are now."

Nebulon began to understand but asked, "What if the physical body or the physical world blocks my vibration? Will I still remain connected to you, Lord?"

"Oh, Nebulon, my gifted one, the same energy I used to create you is the same energy I used to create the physical world. The vibrations and frequencies patterns are different, but the energy that sustains you now will also sustain you in the material world as well."

Nebulon thought for a while and then replied, "Lord, if the vibration and frequency patterns are different, how will I ever know my true self while I am in human form?"

God lovingly smiled and said, "That will be your challenge, Nebulon. I have to make the physical body very dense in order for the physical body to house the powerful energy illumination of the soul. The intellectual body, because it is finite in its nature, will attempt to block the frequency and vibration patterns of the spiritual body. The human mind will have very little or no recollection whatsoever of the unlimited power of its spiritual body."

God paused for just a moment and then finished. "It will be up to the spirit within to awaken the intellectual mind to its existence." God paused once again and then said, "But remember, Nebulon, throughout this entire process, the spiritual you, as you are now, and I will always be connected, even if the physical you denies my existence."

Nebulon's vibration pattern once again accelerated, but God continued, "If the human mind blocks the vibration and frequency patterns of the spiritual mind, then that human being will feel separated from me and the rest of the souls living on Earth. But when the physical mind awakens to its true self while still in human form, the spirit will be enriched. It may take a few human lifetimes before the human mind is awakened, but each lifetime will be a terrific learning experience for the souls who choose to become human."

Nebulon's vibration pattern quickened. "You mean I have to experience life as a human more than once?"

God replied, "Life in the four-dimensional physical world of the Milky Way galaxy will be a very intense physical experience for you. I will create the first human being from the dust of the earth. I will provide all human beings with six senses, five human and one spiritual. I want to ensure that all the souls I have created have the opportunity to experience all the goodness this new world has to offer."

Nebulon was pleased. He had never experienced God becoming so excited about one of his creations. He waited to see if God would continue.

"As a spirit, you can only see and feel love and beauty because I created you and all the others in my likeness and image. You know all there is to know. Your vibrating energy field needs no sustaining. You will never be diminished. You will live forever."

God paused for just a moment and then continued. "When the spirit is born of human flesh, the spirit will have the opportunity to smell, taste, touch, hear, and see as a human being. When the spirit is born of human flesh, the spirit will be given the gift of human emotions. This gift is the link that connects the spirit of God to the spirit of man.

"I call it intuition. When man feels good, he will feel God. When he feels bad, he will call on God for help. The universal law of attraction will sustain all spiritual beings having a human experience. When a human being dies, the spiritual body will return to me. Until the spirit has experienced all human emotions and endeavors, including awakening the human mind and body to its true self, I will continue to design human life plans for each soul."

Nebulon was really excited now. His vibration pattern was all juiced up. "When can I leave for planet Earth, Lord?"

God smiled broadly and said, "Soon, Nebulon. You will be leaving very soon. I am about to create the first human man. I will create him from the dust of the earth and breathe into his nostrils the breath of life, and man will become a living soul. I will call him Adam, the father of the human race. Your human name, Nebulon, will be Noah. The human seed from which you come will be from Adam and his wife, Eve."

Although Nebulon didn't really understand everything God was saying, his love for God was unconditional. He could hardly wait to become a human being named Noah.

Preface

Although the introduction of this book has no scientific proof to back it up, the study of quantum physics has revealed to us that exploring the human body's cellular makeup at the subatomic level is quite an amazing journey. The subatomic particles referred to as quarks are very strange because they are constantly in a state of change.

These hypothetical particles come in several different types (like up, down, charmed, bottom, and strange). Most physicists believe these subatomic particles are held to be constituents of hadrons, which are strong interactions between the different quark particles. What I found very interesting in my research was that even at the subatomic level, these particles have a fractional electrical charge. I wondered if this electrical charge was a field of energy.

In his book The Power of Intention, Wayne Dyer states in chapter one, "As we examine that seed/egg dance attempting to discover its origin, moving backwards toward Creation, we first find molecules, then atoms, then electrons, then subatomic particles, and then sub-subatomic particles. Ultimately, were we to put these tiny quantum subatomic particles into a particle accelerator and collide them, trying to put our finger on the source of life, we'd discover what Einstein and his scientific compatriots discovered: There's no particle at the source; particles do not create more particles. The Source, which is intention, is pure, unbounded energy vibrating so fast that it defies measurement and observation. It's formless energy, and in that formless vibrating spiritual field of energy, intention resides"

I found Dr. Dyer's description of a human birth and spiritual intention enlightening. I wondered if it was possible that every subatomic particle in the material world was like a universe within itself? If that were true, then everything in the material world could have been created by a source of energy so omnipotent that it actually intended you and me to be here. After all, an apple blossom doesn't turn into a pumpkin, and an acorn doesn't grow to become a maple tree. I didn't grow up to be you, and you didn't grow up to me. You and I are uniquely intellectually and physically different, and yet the energy that created us is the same.

For the past twenty-five years, my field of expertise has been in the restaurant industry. My quest was to find the delicate balance between intention versus attraction, risk versus reward, and creative solutions versus proper protection.

The keys that unlock those doors are a secret that has been hidden from the majority of human beings for centuries. The elite have attempted to misdirect, suppress, bury, and hide this secret in order to control their people. Once you understand the secret, it will empower you to apply this knowledge every day. No one will be able to control you.

After I was given the key to unlock the secret, I knew if I had the courage and enough faith to take action, I would begin to live my life on purpose. In doing this I found other keys to other secrets.

I was told by the person who gave me the key to the secret five years ago that I was being entrusted with this information because I had been a truth-seeker all my life and was on a higher level of consciousness. It was to be my destiny to share this information with others.

I was directed to use this information carefully the next four years in an effort to help other people become financially and personally successful.

Ironically, the more successful others became the more successful I became.

I was also told by this person, at the completion of the fourth year of knowing the secret, that if I chose to, I would leave the restaurant industry in order to write books. She stated that during this four-year stint I would find or be given more keys to more secrets—that I would begin to journal this information in a very productive way. I remember smiling to myself, knowing I would never be capable of authoring a book. The idea of writing an entire book seemed way too daunting a task for someone like me.

Then suddenly, in the second year, I began to journal information that I had been researching. As this information began to manifest itself, it seemed natural to not only write it down, but to share it with my supervisors and management teams.

This process continued to spiral upward for the next two years. In October of 2005, I became very aware that my desire to write was overwhelming my ability to focus all my attention on work. I knew the time was approaching rapidly when a decision to write or work had to be made. I would not be allowed to do both. I was brimming over with information that had to be shared with others outside my sphere of influence.

As a result, in January of '06, I left my position with a company that had been paying me well over a six-figure income per year. I had stock options, health benefits, and a solid retirement program. At risk was my family's financial security. The reward would be sharing my journey with you. In my gut, the reward far exceeded the risk.

I will never forget the first day in early January of '06 when I sat down to actually begin the process of writing Living in the Five-Sense World. I was at peace with myself, knowing I had made the correct decision. Although it has been thirteen months since I left my restaurant career, I remain in a state of gratitude, understanding the importance of finishing this project.

It has been illuminating and inspiring to me that throughout the writing process of this book, people who have been searching for information I possess have been sent to me. Although I have never charged anyone for this information, my financial needs continue to be met on a monthly basis.

How is that possible? I have the keys to many secrets that, when applied, allow anyone to tap into resources they didn't know were available to them. Understanding the law of attraction will give you courage. The power of your intention will allow you to embrace your discomfort and tune out any nay-sayers.

Throughout Living in the Five-Sense World, I have left you subtle clues about many secrets. It will be your responsibility to extract this information as it surfaces. My hope is that after you have mastered the secrets, you will want to share those secrets with the people you love.

So snuggle up with a glass of your favorite wine, dim the lights, and read my story. It is my autobiography from August of 1980 to the present. I know you will enjoy discovering the power behind the secrets

Contents

CHAPTER 1
The Cabdriver 1

CHAPTER 2
Insightful yet Frightful 13

CHAPTER 3
An Angel and My Ego 23

CHAPTER 4
Texas Bound and Gagged 25

CHAPTER 5
Set Up for Success or Failure? 30

CHAPTER 6
Neo-Tech Man 32

CHAPTER 7
Unexpected Surprises 39

CHAPTER 8
Coincidence or Certainty? 49

Chapter 9
　The Land of Entrapment 51

Chapter 10
　The Golden Boy 55

Chapter 11
　Open Your Mind, Attaching It to No-Thing 57

Chapter 12
　The Reading 61

Chapter 13
　Opportunity knocking.. 66

Chapter 14
　News Flash – My New Discovery 72

Chapter 15
　Curiosity, Faith, Belief, Knowing 78

Chapter 16
　Ya gotta be ready when you go to Gallup 88

Chapter 17
　The Dark-Haired Woman Arrives 93

Chapter 18
　La Cruces, New Mexico 97

Chapter 19
　Bill Arrives from California 110

Chapter 20
　Snow, Ghosts, and a Revelation 130

Chapter 21
　The Rest of the Story 139

Chapter 22
　The Final Chapter 162

CHAPTER 1
The Cabdriver

It was late August 1980, the hottest summer on record in Dallas/ Fort Worth, Texas. I recall over a hundred straight days with temperatures soaring over the hundred-degree mark. It seemed no matter what you did or where you went, being outside was miserable.

Earlier in the year, I had decided to change my career path. During the previous two years, I had been working in the restaurant industry. I thought my prior military experience would be a good fit. I found out my authoritative methods did not work so well on civilians. Attending management seminars and reading books about how to manage people vastly improved my methods.

For almost two years, I had been an assistant manager for Long John Silver's. Being young, restless, and in a big hurry to be successful, I thought I was ready to manage my own restaurant. I felt I was being overlooked. I gave my proper notice and changed my career path

I applied for a manufacturing engineering position at Texas Instruments in Lewisville, Texas and was hired on the spot. Although I accepted less money than I was making, I didn't think this would pose a major financial problem, but it did.

I was married and had four young children, a house payment, and plenty of bills, and I was working for less money. My wife decided to try to take some of the burden off of me by caring for children in our home. Even with the additional income she raised, at the end of the month there was always more month than money.

It finally got to the point that I had no choice but to borrow quite a sum of money from my brother in order to catch up. He was a very good businessman, so he structured a deal that would insure his money was safe.

He suggested I drive one of his taxi cabs at night and all day on the weekends until the debt was retired. Except for the long hours, I discovered I really enjoyed driving cab. The stories I could tell you are amazing.

As a matter of fact, I had an experience while driving cab that was so unique and powerful it not only powered up my inner software for years, but inspired the title to the first chapter of this book. Although I dismissed my baptism into the world of the unknown, the seed of curiosity was firmly planted in my subconscious.

I remember it was a Saturday. I pulled into the cab stand at Love Field. I looked around and saw one of the cabdrivers I knew standing in the shade outside the terminal. Although I knew him pretty well, for some weird reason his name has been blocked from my memory, and yet the conversation we had that day in late August I have never forgotten.

I hardly remember what he looked like back then. All I recall is he was an older guy with wavy black hair speckled with gray. He was average in height, stocky, and yet mild-mannered. Meek, I suppose, would best describe his personality.

I got out of my cab and walked over to him.

"Top of the morning to you, Kev," he said.

I told him good morning and asked how he was doing. We then began to play some mental gymnastics, which was normal for him. Then the conversation began to get a little strange. For a reason that was not clear to me at the time, our discussion made a shift into the realm of the metaphysical.

This gentle soul started to discuss with me energy and how it affects the way we live. He tried to explain to me how this energy worked and what it was comprised of. In 1980 the most I understood about energy was terms like inertia and kinetic. Matter is either at rest or in motion. When in motion, matter changes and transfers energy into heat. His perspective was much more esoteric—almost mystical in nature. I was uncomfortable with what he was saying while in the same moment terribly fascinated and curious. I wondered where this was going and if I really wanted to go there.

He told me God was nothing but a pure form of energy. Everything we know in the material world is created by this energy and this form of energy had many different vibrations. He stated, "The same energy that grows your hair and fingernails is also contained in pictures, music, and your thoughts. The vibration patterns are different, but it is the same energy."

I remember thinking that this seemed kind of airy-fairy. To be perfectly honest, that's what I told him. His response was enthusiastic to say the least.

"Let's take this idea you have of airy-fairy and put it to a test," he expounded. "Let's talk about thought energy and see how it works." Not waiting for me to object, he began, "Thoughts are very fast-moving energy.

When one learns to keep one's thoughts in order, his thoughts become centered and aligned with the universe. When this happens, all things are possible."

At this point I had to stop him. "You are beginning to sound like a Zen monk," I explained.

His smile broadened. "You want proof?"

I must have had a pretty stupid look on my face and said something like, "How in the world can you prove to me your thoughts are aligned with the universe?"

He was now laughing. "Do you understand the concept of manifesting?"

I said, "Maybe not in the same context you are referring to."

He said, "You are probably right. Let me explain. We who are surviving on planet Earth live by our five senses. If we can't see it, touch it, hear it, smell it, or taste it, it does not exist. Manifesting your thoughts goes beyond the five-sense world into a realm of faith, connecting the physical self to one's higher self. In doing this you can manifest and then project that thought back into the material world. The Bible refers to this as 'ask and you shall receive.'"

I told him I understood the concept of faith and the idea of asking to receive, but all the other stuff was very confusing.

He ignored my comment and patiently proceeded forward. "All human thoughts have different vibration patterns. That vibration pattern manifests into the collective consciousness of universal thought. The secret is connecting the physical you with the spiritual you."

I asked, "So, this like praying?"

"Yeah, sort of." He smiled. "It's like a prayer on steroids. One that is supercharged. When you learn you can do this and trust in it—and you will—you can live each and every day from that day forward in amazement. Now for your proof!" he stated boldly. "Do you see the old man sitting on the bench over there, reading the paper?" he asked.

I nodded quickly.

"I am going to close my eyes and project my thought energy around him and manifest a pesky fly buzzing around his head. He will continue reading his paper; however, he will begin to swat at what he believes is a fly buzzing around him." He then closed his eyes. Within fifteen seconds, this old man began to swat at an invisible fly! I was dumbfounded. This seemingly meek, well-mannered cabdriver had just pulled off the best magic trick ever. Here was an old man sitting on a bench less than twenty feet away, swatting a fly that didn't exist. Wow!

He opened his eyes and asked me what I had seen. I told him I had watched as the old man continued to read his paper and then began to swat at a fly. He smiled and said, "Now do you understand?"

I did not respond. I walked briskly over to the old man and said, "Excuse me, sir. I hate to bother you, but do you see the man standing over there by the terminal?"

He stated he did. I asked him if he knew him. He said he did not. I thanked him for his time and walked back to the cabdriver.

As I approached him, he said, "I see we have a doubting Thomas to deal with!"

I retorted, "So what's the trick?"

"Kev, there is no trick," he clamored. "I will give you just one more opportunity to get this. Come with me."

We walked down the terminal until we reached a large picture window. He said, "Tell me what you see."

I told him I saw a female ticket agent in the process of typing up tickets for waiting passengers. Her back was to us, but she looked really busy.

He asked, "How many passengers do you see waiting in line?"

I told him there were seven.

"That is perfect!" he responded.

"Now I am going to close my eyes and again project my thought energy, which will surround her. Soul to soul, I will ask her to stop what she is doing, turn around, smile, and wave at you. Got it?"

He smiled and winked at me. I was speechless and could only nod my head in agreement. He slowly closed his eyes, and within fifteen seconds the girl stopped what she was doing, turned around, smiled, and waved at me. I managed to smile and wave back at her. I was absolutely bewildered. He once again opened his eyes and asked what I had seen. I told him what I had seen was exactly what he had said I would. He then asked me again, "Do you understand?"

Backing up slowly, I told him I understood he was the most dangerous man on the planet!

I went back to my cab and drove to DFW airport. I never saw him again. I did not speak about this experience to anyone for sixteen years. What happened that day did not fit into my value system, principles, or religious upbringing. I certainly was not ready or prepared to accept this multidimensional, paranormal spirituality—this no-nonsense way of living my life. I was totally okay in working things out the old-fashioned way: hard work, long hours, and my trusted five senses. Life sucks from time to time. We all know this and feel okay accepting that fact, right? I guess what I mean; we all have our good days and bad days. This is our reality. Besides, I believed mind control was very dangerous and should not be messed around with.

1981 through 1984

From 1981 to 1984, both my personal life and career were pretty much in the toilet. I bought self-help books and tapes. Nothing seemed to help.

In the fall of 1984, my marriage appeared to be over. My wife and I had separated. I remember being so depressed I could hardly get out of bed. I finally decided if I couldn't have my Earthly home I would take my chances on the other side. There was no light whatsoever at the end of my tunnel. Imagine, if you can, the darkest shade of black you have ever experienced: pitch black.

No color, no light, and nothing to look forward to but hopelessness: this, my friend, is a description of a suicide about to happen. I remember it vividly because I was there, prepared, and ready to make it happen. I was exhausted, perplexed, confused, and literally looking down the barrel of a .45 semiautomatic pistol and feeling very peaceful about my future.

Being judgmental, I had always considered someone who committed suicide a person I would have labeled as a coward for running away from his problems. I no longer feel this way. The act of suicide is an act of quiet desperation. It takes courage to end one's life. What causes a person to become suicidal? I feel that a person who commits the act of suicide is able to disconnect from reality. He or she experiences an emotional blowout. To fully understand this act of selfishness, one must come to the brink without actually going over it.

Miraculously in my case, the emotional blowout didn't totally disconnect me from reality. I was able to realize the emotional damage I would have created for the people I loved might never have been repaired. I became aware that ending my life was not to be my legacy. I would stay the course unselfishly.

1985 through 1990

From 1985 to 1990, I decided to reenter the restaurant industry. Besides reading self-help books, I had also added to my collection many books on leadership. I found myself back again with Long John Silver's, this time enrolled in their fast-track manager's program. It wouldn't be long before I would get the opportunity to manage my first restaurant.

During my four-year stint with LJS, I managed two restaurants. In 1987, I became a certified stage-one–training store manager. This was a highly respected position because of the demands and expectations that were required of not only the training manager but also the entire staff. Three weeks out of every month, four manager trainees would arrive. They knew absolutely nothing about LJS. It was our job to break them in and my responsibility to evaluate their performances on a daily and weekly basis. We took enormous pride in exceeding those expectations. It was a pretty normal occurrence when the regional training coordinator would find out about a supervisor putting off hiring someone until he knew when my next class would be available. There were certainly other training stores; however, the supervisors knew we would treat their folks professionally and I would provide them with accurate feedback.

In 1989, I received an award for "manager of the year." This was the highest, most prestigious award a manager could receive from the Long John Silver's community. The award reflected excellence in all aspects of the manager's restaurant. This recognition could not possibly be obtained without a tremendous supporting cast, which I was fortunate to have.

In late 1989, the company was in the process of a leverage buyout. The changes were so dramatic that by March of 1990 I decided to leave the organization. It was one of the saddest days of my life.

I decided to open my own business. I showed my well-thought-out business plan to everyone I respected in the business world. They all thought the business plan was exceptional.

Then I got to thinking about my metaphysical cabdriver friend. What if this stuff he talked about was for real! Wouldn't a smart man ensure that all of his bases were covered? I thought it certainly couldn't hurt to check it out.

I looked in the Fort Worth phone book under the heading of psychics. I was surprised that there were several listings. Even though I had very little understanding and much less faith in what I was about to do, I did it anyway.

I picked up the phone and soon had an appointment to get a spiritual reading.

I went over to a lady's house and knocked on the door. A very beautiful lady, obviously from India, answered the door and very politely invited me in. The house was nicely furnished with a Eastern flair. The air was slightly scented with a very subtle hint of rosemary coming from an incense burner in the corner of the room. I recall feeling how peaceful the environment was. She gently took my hand and guided me to a table where I assumed the reading would take place. There were many types of candles of different shapes, sizes, and colors sitting on the table. Also on the table was a strange-looking deck of cards. She handed me the cards and asked if I would shuffle the deck while she lit the candles. I told her I would be happy to. She explained to me that after she was finished lighting the candles and I was through shuffling the cards, the reading would begin. She then told me the cards I was shuffling were called tarot cards. Like most decks of cards, they were plain on one side and on the reverse side there were many different kinds of people symbols with vague explanations at the top and bottom of each card. I had never seen anything like them before.

I finished shuffling the deck and handed it back to her. She closed her eyes in prayer, asking God permission to grant her guidance in the reading she was about to give to me. She began to lay the cards down on the table. She smiled the most loving smile and asked me what I wanted to know. I was a bit unprepared for this, so I kind of stumbled a bit but recovered nicely. "I just need to know one thing and only one thing," I blurted out.

She continued smiling and laying down the cards. "And that one thing would be?" she asked.

"Am I going to make a lot of money in the future?" I stammered.

She looked at me very seriously for a long moment and then very sweetly she said, "Absolutely! You are destined to make a lot of money"

As the saying goes, I was smiling from ear to ear. I paid her my twenty bucks, thanked her for her time, and bounded down her porch steps. I not only had the approval of the best people I knew in the business community, more importantly, I felt I had God's approval too. All I had to do was find a partner.

I found my partner, we put our money together, and within ninety days I was broke and overextended. I had little choice but to file personal and corporate bankruptcy. I was able to return half the money my partner had invested in the business, but my own personal finances were in shambles. Oh well. So much for approval. What really puzzled me was what the spiritual reader had told me, "You are destined to make a lot of money." I realized later that when one speaks to spiritual advisors, one must be very specific with one's questions.

She was correct in her reading. Six years later, I did begin to make a lot of money. If I had asked her whether my business venture would be a success, I am certain she would have steered me away from that venture.

From the time my business failed until mid-1996, there were many ups and downs. I went back to work in the restaurant business. I was involved with Wendy's International for about a year and half. Then I took an opportunity to become a working partner for Golden Corral in Farmington, New Mexico. That lasted about eight months. The restaurant was doing great and I was making more money than I ever had before, but moving the family from Dallas/Fort Worth to Farmington, New Mexico was a culture shock for the younger family members. It seemed to me I spent a lot of my time at the principal's office.

The kid's just didn't want to stay in school.

I also kept receiving phone calls from my former regional vice president with Long John Silvers, Henry Proctor. He had left LJS before the buyout and had gone to work with SONIC Drive-In. The franchisee he was involved with was in the process of building a SONIC restaurant in Ocala, Florida. He was doing his best to entice me to come on board.

He and I had actually discussed this opportunity prior to my involvement with Golden Corral; however, at that time, the group had not even purchased the land on which to build the restaurant. They had speculated on a lot, so my wife and I decided to drive down to Ocala to take a look at the property they were contemplating buying. It was my opinion the lot they were looking at buying was in the wrong part of Ocala. It was located on the main road leaving Ocala to go to Daytona Beach, but that was the only positive attribute the property had besides a solid residential base. In the restaurant business, the location of a new restaurant is not only critical to your success, but should be critical to your expectations as well.

I had two concerns relating to the property. First, there was no commercial development around the location, which meant very little draw for breakfast and lunch. Secondly, the lot was way below street level, which also meant additional money would have to be spent to buy tons of fill dirt to raise the drive-in so it could be seen from the street. And although the land was reasonably priced, the additional improvement to the lot would make the deal less desirable. For a few more bucks, they could have bought property on what was referred to then as restaurant row, in downtown Ocala.

My last concern was marketing. SONIC was a regional company at this juncture. Most folks in Florida would have never heard of the concept. Local store marketing would only have so much reach. Additional money would have to be budgeted for local TV, and print ads if the restaurant was going to succeed.

My original decision to work for Golden Corral and not SONIC was based on the fact they were at least nine months away from opening their restaurant, and the theory was that when they did, they might not succeed.

As I mentioned previously, everything at the Corral was going very well. Other than keeping my three youngest children in school, I was happy.

Then I met Bobby Merritt. He was and still is a SONIC Drive-In franchisee out of Las Cruces, New Mexico. One evening, Bobby and Ted Sprinkle (supervisor for Bobby in the Farmington market) had dinner at the Corral. I had a good visit with them and agreed to dine with them the following evening. Ted said he wanted to bring his wife, Sherry, and I agreed to bring my wife, Cindy.

Little did I realize how family-oriented the SONIC Drive-In family was. The Golden Corral believed in nepotism but SONIC took that concept to heights that are still undiscovered by most restaurant chains. When I say that back then SONIC was a mom-and-pop business, I mean just that. Husbands and wives were the working partners and one or the other was expected to be in the store at all times. Total commitment to the organization and the brand was the name of the game. For a nominal investment, a restaurant manager could become a partner and share in the profits of the restaurant. If a partner had children who were old enough to work, they too could work at the drive-in.

The following evening, Cindy and I met with Bobby, Ted, and Sherry. We found out Bobby was involved with the Ocala, Florida deal. Nine months prior I had met Darrell Rogers, the other franchisee who would be involved in Florida. So now I knew who all the players were: Henry, Bobby, and Darrell. Both Bobby and Darrell appeared to have very successful organizations. Combined, they controlled well over a hundred restaurants.

Darrell was very proud that his organization's average unit volume was over a million dollars, and Bobby was, and still is, the largest single owner franchisee in the SONIC system. Henry's reputation was impeccable.

Needless to say, with all the credentials these three fellows had, my ego was being stroked pretty hard knowing they wanted me to partner up with them in Florida. They each felt I had the knowledge and ability to become a huge success within the world of SONIC. I was not convinced just yet.

After a very nice dinner filled with wonderful conversations with Bobby, Ted, and his lovely wife Sherry, we left.

On the way home, I asked Cindy what she thought. She said she felt like it should be a family decision. I agreed. It seemed to both of us we had just gotten settled in Farmington. How could we possibly think about uprooting the entire family again so soon and moving to Florida? No matter how good the opportunity appeared to be, it seemed a little crazy to both of us. This decision would have to be made by the entire family.

The family input was of value; however, their support in moving across the country and their willingness to learn an entirely different restaurant concept would be critical to everyone's success.

CHAPTER 2
Insightful yet Frightful

After much thought and many family discussions, the decision to go to Ocala, Florida was finalized. The concerns I had about the location, marketing agenda, and the additional construction expenses had been quelled through the conversations I had with Henry Proctor. I trusted his judgment and business savvy. Henry had been responsible for over 125 Long John Silver restaurants. Bobby Merritt and Darrell Rogers had started from scratch and now controlled over one hundred restaurants. I was in no position to question their professional judgment.

They each felt this location was going to be a winner. Done deal!

They put a typical financial package together. The partnership would pay for our move from Farmington, New Mexico to Ocala, Florida and provide health and life insurance plus a small salary of two thousand dollars per month. In addition, I would be allowed to enter into a limited partnership with Bobby, Darrell, and Henry. Per this agreement, I would be allowed to purchase 20 percent of the restaurant's potential profit; however, I would not own any of the building, land, depreciation, or equipment. This seemed fair; however, it was very important to me that if this venture was successful, I ensured I didn't get trapped in one location. I was able to negotiate for some additional ownership in future drive-ins and a promotion to supervisor after we had successfully opened a total of six restaurants. I believe this was met with very little resistance only because the SONIC group was feeling a lot of pressure, stemming from the fact that the drive-in was nearing completion and they had not been able to put a management team together. It was mid-April and restaurant's projected opening date was in mid-May.

Bells and whistles, alarms and red flags should have been going off and flying around my head. And they probably were; I just didn't see or hear them. I was so impressed with these guys and so confident in my family and my own abilities I never saw what might happen. As in most dysfunctional relationships, the marriage could be over shortly after the honeymoon.

I was pressured into giving Golden Corral a one-week notice. In the restaurant business this can be an act of suicide, because if things didn't work out with SONIC, I might miss out on the opportunity to work for Golden Corral again because I gave them such a short notice.

My eldest son, Kevin Jr., and I left the family in Farmington and headed to Tyler, Texas for a week's worth of SONIC training. The rest of the family packed up our household goods and waited on the movers, after which they would drive to Tyler, Texas; hookup with us; and then we would all caravan down to Ocala, Florida.

It took two days to get from Tyler, Texas to Ocala, Florida. We arrived late in the afternoon on the second day and went straight to the restaurant. I have to admit that from the outside it was a beautiful store. The group didn't pinch any pennies pulling this one out of the ground.

The drive-in restaurant was perpendicular to the main road used to access the restaurant. Pulling into the restaurant, a guest would be greeted by an abundance of magnificent flowerbeds that were strategically organized in a horizontal fashion, running perpendicular to the front of the store. Also in the front was an oversized covered patio with enough outside seating for twenty-four people. The entire lot was finished in white concrete, no asphalt. Thirty stalls were adorned with the most beautiful menu housings I had ever seen.

The perimeter of the lot was filled with green shrubs of different heights and widths. There was also an uncovered patio opposite the drive-thru window.

Surrounding that patio were more flowers, shrubs, stones, rocks, and trees. The outside of the building was finished in tan stucco. What really appealed to me was the elevation of the property. From the rear of the property to the front of the property, there was just a slight grade difference. It would make it easy for the carhops to skate in either direction.

That first night we turned on the outside lights to include all the neon. My goodness, what a site to behold! Flaming red and bright-yellow neon split the darkness that night, which could only be described as "viva Las Vegas."

The outside perimeter of the canopy and the top of the building were double banded with one red and one yellow strip of neon.

Underneath the canopy were an enormous amount of florescent light bulbs. They provided so much white light that even though it was pitch black all around us, it appeared to be high noon at SONIC.

The menu housings, which are placed at car window heights, were attached to the poles that supported the canopy. They also were illuminated but with much smaller U-shaped florescent light bulbs. I was certain we could be seen not only from the main street, but perhaps from planet Jupiter as well. It was so dramatic; people began to pull into the lot, hoping we were open. We provided all of them with bounce-back coupons and thanked them for stopping by. We informed them that our restaurant's grand opening was a week away but reminded them that was just an estimate.

There was a tremendous amount of work to be done and only my family to ensure it got done. I was amazed; Henry had not hired any hourly employees. In addition to getting the restaurant ready to open, Kevin Jr. and I would have to hire all the employees and get them ready for the trainers.

Even after driving all day and arriving late in the afternoon, we all worked till after midnight that first day. The next morning, we were all at the restaurant by 7:00 a.m. and worked until after midnight that day too. This routine continued till we opened seven days from when we had arrived.

If you have never had the chance to open a restaurant or perhaps have never worked in a restaurant, you may not fully appreciate the amount of time, energy, dedication, teamwork, organization, and planning it requires to maintain your sanity when you are under that kind of pressure.

Fortunately Cindy and our children handled the pressure and dedicated themselves to getting the job done like seasoned pros.

For example, the household goods were delivered the third day after our arrival in Ocala. It was three weeks after we opened the restaurant before any one of us would take time off to begin unpacking our belongings.

We unpacked stuff as the need arose. Nobody complained about the long hours or the many tasks they were asked to perform. No father was more proud of his wife, sons, and daughters than I was. Their personal sacrifices will always be remembered, cherished, and appreciated.

During the first week, Kevin and I hired hundred and twenty employees and brought in trainers from all over the country. With fingers crossed, we all held our breath, said a prayer, and then opened the restaurant.

Opening a new business is like waiting on your wife to give birth to a child.

You never know how people are going to respond to your creation. Fortunately, the people who lived in Ocala liked our creation. They were beating our doors down, and we responded with organized chaos. The trainers did a magnificent job, considering none of our employees had any SONIC experience.

Within a week the first set of trainers were sent home and a second group of trainers arrived. The second group of trainers continued the excellent training that the first group of trainers had begun. I had never seen so much dedication from so many people in all my years in this business.

They not only trained my staff hands-on but provided my management team with excellent feedback on key employees. Most of the trainers commented about the extraordinary number of exceptional employees we were able to employ in such a short period of time. I felt like this was a direct reflection of the quality of the folks living within a two-mile radius of the restaurant. I knew that in the future, cutting the staff back to a normal size would be a real challenge.

This task is never easy or pleasant. It takes a great deal of time, discipline, feedback, and awareness. Evaluations should be done daily. Admittedly, with a 120 employees to evaluate daily, some of the part-time staff were not receiving as much feedback as preferred. So I personally took on the responsibility of evaluating their performances.

Then the first of June arrived and something extraordinary occurred. The daily store sales headed south, seemingly overnight. As I reviewed the same day's sales for the previous week, it became obvious we were trending down.

This situation always happens, but it is not normal for it to happen so quickly.

I brought this to the attention of Henry Proctor, who didn't seem to be overly concerned. I told him that I felt this was unusual and something must have happened to warrant this. He appeared to be distracted, so I let it go for the time being.

The daily sales continued to trend down every week in the month of June when compared to the previous week. My continued hope was the daily sales would bottom out soon, because if we continued trending down, this situation was going to get really serious in a hurry. Additionally, we were spending an excessive amount of money on labor. Cutting the staff back was becoming imperative. During the second week in June, I had no choice but to try to find a balance. Our profitability would depend on it.

By mid-June, I was still curious and plagued by the reoccurring thought of declining sales. In my opinion, operationally we were sound. I felt we were exceeding our guest's expectations on a daily basis. As a footnote, I must state I never based this feeling on just the tools that were available to assist myself in determining operational excellence. For instance, you can't measure crew morale; you have to feel it. I made it a point every day to determine what state of mind each person was in. It is very important to do this, because cutting back the staff, if not properly handled, could have had a long-term, powerful, and negative impact on not only the community and the employees leaving but also on the employees remaining.

It has been said and verified that an employee who is fired unjustly can cause a business more grief than a customer who is mistreated. The rationale behind this concept is that the unemployed worker has the inside scoop on you. If an employee feels he was fired unjustly, he may decide to demonize you or your business. If an employee had a concern or issue, together we would find some mutual form of resolution.

Over the years I had come to understand that happy and secure people develop into highly productive team players. My style of managing people demanded I go to great lengths in order to ensure the folks I was responsible for were happy and feeling like their contributions were appreciated.

With that said, I was convinced the employees were not a factor in the declining of sales. We were serving quality fresh, food in a fast, friendly, and helpful manner on a day-to-day basis. Our guests knew what to expect when they drove on the lot. The only way to actually verify their personal satisfaction was for management to get out on the lot and ask them questions pertaining to their SONIC experience. Without exception, the feedback I received was very positive. Even when we made mistakes, we were able to resolve them quickly and professionally. If our guests were happy and satisfied, then why were we trending down in sales? I noticed much of the decline was occurring during two of the main day parts: lunch and happy hour. I wondered if this was perhaps weather related.

It was summertime in Ocala, Florida. Every day was the same: searing heat and stifling humidity. It rained every day at three o'clock in the afternoon. As they say, you could set your watch by it. I remember the rain hitting the asphalt and concrete; immediately changing into a steam vapor. If you walked outside, you'd start to sweat like an old man eating a jalapeño pepper.

I thought it possible most folks didn't want to be eating hot food in their cars this time of the year. Maybe we'd just have to muddle through the summer.

By mid-July we were still in a sales decline. That's about the time the finger-pointing began. Bobby's philosophy was very different than Darrell's, and yet they agreed on one thing. Operationally they thought the store had problems. They were both convinced the sales decline was due to our inability to execute. Bobby felt we were too fast and not serving quality food and Darrell's perception was we were not fast enough.

Darrell brought in one of his supervisors to evaluate the operation of the restaurant. I was actually excited about this when I got wind they were coming to Ocala. Since neither Henry nor I had very much experience with SONIC, I thought his input might be a tremendous help. Maybe this guy would have a silver bullet that could turn this thing around. It didn't take long for me to realize that this guy was not the Lone Ranger.

I was convinced after I heard his evaluation that operationally we had a difference of opinion. The supervisor's unfair and bizarre evaluation made me think that perhaps my days were numbered. I will not even honor this experience with an explanation of what actually transpired those two days, except to say he turned out to be Darrell's hit man.

July's sales were less than June's. Since we were still trending down, I convinced Henry our sales issues were twofold. Through my discussions with the local business people in Ocala, I discovered that around the first of June, a very large segment of the population, especially in the neighborhood we were in, head north for the summer. They are referred to as snow birds. They leave in June and start to come back toward the end of August. I now understood the reason for the quick sales decline in June. The other side of the coin was the lack of time and money we had spent advertising our business. Henry volunteered to get outside the store and do some local store marketing.

It worked like a charm. By the end of August we had surpassed the sales we had made in July. This meant possibly we had finally leveled off.

On September 1, I was surprised to see Bobby and Darrell. I could hardly wait to tell them the good news. I felt they would be very pleased. Good news had been hard to come by the previous sixty days. But what happened instead was so sneaky and so well camouflaged I never saw it coming.

I was called outside to the patio area across from the drive-thru window. Henry and Bobby were talking, and Darrell was rustling through some papers he was looking over. Everyone appeared to be in a good mood. I greeted them and they responded cordially. I sat in the only spot available, which was directly across from Darrell. There was some small talk, and then Darrell dropped the bomb. Looking directly at me, very nonchalantly he stated that Bobby and he had decided to dissolve the partnership. I was so stunned all I could muster was "What does that mean?" Of course I knew what it meant.

I had been fired and so had Henry. Case closed! Darrell was very quick to confirm that the honeymoon and the marriage were over.

My head was spinning with numerous thoughts of the past, present, and of course my future. I had never been fired before. I didn't know how to react or respond, so for a while I just listened. I do remember asking about the money I had invested, which at that moment seemed to be a logical question. Darrell's response was "Your money has been spent!" If I had known then what I know now, I would not have signed the documents Darrell put in front of me. If they had wanted to dissolve the partnership, they should have bought out my interest. I suspect they bought out Henry but I don't know. He was in his fifties. In this business it would have been very difficult for him to find another organization willing to invest in him, so he would have needed the resources that would have tied him over until that occurred. It is sad to say, but Henry Proctor and I have not spoken a word to each other since that day. We just went our separate ways.

I recall getting up from the table and glancing over at Bobby. He appeared to me to be really sad about all this. They say the eyes are the windows of the soul. As our eyes met, I felt I was looking directly into Bobby's soul and it was telling me that this was a gut-wrenching experience for him too. In that fleeting moment, I realized this had been Darrell's deal. I took some comfort in realizing that perhaps Bobby knew how much my family had given up to take on this business venture, and perhaps it was bothering him.

I walked away and then stopped. I went back to the table. I warned them that if I couldn't turn this restaurant around, nobody could. And it wouldn't matter who they brought in to replace me; they would wind up closing the restaurant.

In May 1996 they served their last burger. When I found out about it, all I felt was sadness. My family had sacrificed its time and energy for that SONIC Drive-In, and for what purpose?

Even though I was upset when I made the prediction that this restaurant would ultimately fail, it would be years before I would recognize my ability to predict future outcomes and future events based on what I was feeling instinctively rather than thinking and having to analyze them.

It would become very clear; my path was never meant to include Florida.

Sometimes lessons are meant to be learned and free will ensures we learn them.

Here are some lessons I learned:

(1) Never work for more than one franchisee.
(2) Never let a group of people stroke your ego, talking you into making a critical life decision though the little voice inside you is screaming, "It is too good to be true."

(3) When going into a business venture with others, you better own at least 51 percent of the deal or you can become at risk in a hurry.

(4) Never sacrifice your family's dignity for someone else's ego.

(5) Never commit all your trust, resources, or productivity to anyone who does not commit a tremendous amount of his or her energy and time building permanent relationships.

(6) Never be afraid of failure and you will breed success.

(7) Be principled in the face of adversity. Admit when you are wrong but maintain your composure.

(8) Maintain your emotional state of well-being. Never get too high or too low. It clouds your decision-making ability.

(9) If you close your eyes and remain silent, calming your mind, and listen, you will be able to hear one door closing and the next door opening.

Chapter 3
An Angel and My Ego

Most people living in the five-sense world would have had a similar reaction to getting fired from their job as I did: embarrassed, stressed, frustrated, angry, resentful, untrusting, and very discouraged. I now know these feelings are negative energies and can be bad for the physical and intellectual bodies.

A secret I would learn years later is that human emotion is actually a gift. The emotional body is like a barometer. At any given moment we can measure how we are feeling. Emotions assist us in remapping our reality.

Ten days after the partnership had been dissolved; my ego was still so inflamed I would not ask my former partners for help in finding a position with another concept. What made it even more difficult for me was watching the entire family leave the house to go to work every day at the SONIC Drive-In. I think Bobby and Darrell realized the family would be professional enough to support the new partner and were all well liked and accepted by the current staff. I would just have to take my ego and stick in my back pocket and deal with it.

Within Darrell's organization there was an angel. I was at a low ebb one day when I received a call from James Junkin, the director of operations for Darrell's group. James and I had known each other since the late '70s.

He gave me the phone number to John Willingham, who was now the director of operations for Restaurant Management Corporation (RMC) out of Albuquerque, New Mexico. RMC operated Pizza Huts, Grandy's Chicken, and Long John Silver's concepts. The really neat thing about this situation was that John Willingham had been my area supervisor when I had worked for Long John Silver's in the '70s. I immediately gave him a call.

To make a long story short, the next day RMC flew me to Dallas to meet with John. Picture this: I was sitting in a Chili's restaurant just outside the Dallas/Fort Worth airport with a man who not only knew my reputation with LJS but was also a trusted friend. Maybe God does work in mysterious ways.

John and I reminisced for a while and then he offered me a position managing a brand new Long John Silver's they were going to build in Copperas Cove, Texas. Bam! I was back in Texas. I didn't even know were Copperas Cove, Texas was. Guess what? I didn't care, either. All I needed to know was that soon we would be getting out of Florida and I would get as far away from SONIC as I could.

I was offered a reasonable salary with a very nice benefit package. John also offered to pay for my moving expenses. We shook hands and the deal was done. I caught my return flight to Florida, and the rest was soon to become history.

Chapter 4
Texas Bound and Gagged

As unbelievable as this is going to sound, the family was allowed to continue working at the SONIC in Ocala, Florida while I was back in Texas overseeing the construction of the new Long John Silver's. The partner/manager, Bobby and Darrell, brought in was one of Darrell's gunslingers from Tyler, Texas.

Sound familiar to you? As you'll remember, I spent a week with this guy getting my feet wet with SONIC. I really liked him and apparently he liked my family too. When he found out we would be moving back to Texas, he could have immediately hired some new folks and terminated them. But he didn't do that. He instead managed the situation like a pro. I have always felt a great appreciation for John Tyler's ability to work around the family schedules and moving timeframes.

Kevin Jr. decided to stay in Florida and work with John Tyler, titled as an assistant manager. This was a big decision for him for two reasons. First, was this the career he wanted? And secondly, he realized the rest of the family would be moving on and leaving him behind.

We spent the last night together as a family at Kevin's new apartment. The next day we left for Texas. I remember thinking, as we drove away, how quickly time passes. It seemed like it was only yesterday that I was carrying this young boy around on my shoulders. And now as I looked in my rearview mirror, I watched as this tall, handsome, intelligent young man stood, waving goodbye to the only family he had known. I knew he was ready to meet life head on, but I suppose it is hard for all parents to let go. I was no exception.

I now know that when you are living your life in a lower state of consciousness, life isn't always how you perceive or envision it to be. At the time I personally had no clue how all of this would turn out. What I did know was that I would miss him terribly, as would the rest of the family members.

Amazingly, history would prove he made the right decision.

During our stint in Copperas Cove, Texas, life continued to be full of fun and challenges. Our eldest daughter, Misty, graduated from high school and then decided to get married. Although I was not happy about this, I had learned to try not to give advice when I felt it was not appreciated. After all, who was I to get in the way of another person's life lessons.

Her future husband was very handsome and appeared to really care for her, but my gut was telling me something was not right. It did not take long before Misty came to the same conclusions, but not before she conceived a child.

Interesting enough, she divorced him and married his older brother, who, by the way, was the brother she should have married in the first place. James and Misty have had two more boys since then and are happily married, living in Cheyenne, Wyoming. Her firstborn, Clayton, is living with them too.

Through all of this, her husband and his family, to include the other brother Steve, have remained close and very supportive.

As a parent it was hard to be an observer when all this was going on. All we could do was trust Misty's instincts, try to support her decisions, and love her unconditionally. Staying out of our children's business has proven to be a formula that usually provides for success.

Meanwhile, our other daughter, Tonya, thought she was in love with an army guy from Fort Hood and decided to move in with him. Seriously, I really liked her boyfriend, but deep down, I felt like this was not going to be a long-term relationship.

Kevin Jr. stayed in Florida for a period of time and then Bobby Merritt offered him a partnership in Los Alamos, New Mexico. He stopped by on his way to New Mexico. He looked great and was really excited about the opportunity Bobby was giving him. I thought, *Man, he is awfully young to be given all this responsibility.* I should have realized how many phone calls I would be getting on a daily basis. Sometimes I felt like I was managing one restaurant and supervising another. Actually I enjoyed sharing my knowledge with him because he never asked the same question twice. Not surprisingly, he was a quick and very astute learner.

What did surprise me one day was a call from Bobby Merritt, wondering if I would be interested in coming back to work for SONIC. What an interesting conversation we had. I was somewhat shocked he would take the time to call me. I tried to be as polite as I could, but I had no interest in ever working for SONIC Drive-Ins now or in the future. I was still upset about the treatment I had received in Florida

Our youngest son, Justin, was having a wonderful time getting in trouble and not going to school, which was his forte. He was a good kid and fun to be around; he just enjoyed breaking any rule you put in front of him. He was like a young stallion that couldn't be corralled. He never thought things through before he did them. He would just do them and then suffer the logical consequences.

We bought a house on five acres of land. We were convinced this was the home and the area we would retire to. The restaurant was doing well, my reputation was restored, and we knew all the right people in town. Life was really beginning to feel good again. My world was in a state of calmness.

We had been in the house a little over a year when I received a phone call from John Willingham, requesting I move to Albuquerque, New Mexico.

This was not a promotion, just a lateral move. I would be performing the same duties I was currently executing. I would just be tasking in a different part of the country. My compensation would stay the same.

I was informed by John that a restaurant that had been doing very well over the past couple of years was now in a steady sales decline. Upper management felt like it was a management issue. I would be replacing the current general manager. Does this situation sound at all familiar to you?

My reputation among Long John Silver's upper management was very similar to how the SONIC owners felt about John Tyler, who, if you remember, was the partner/manager that replaced me in Ocala, Florida.

I, like John Tyler with SONIC, had spent most of my career with Long John Silver's, fixing and repairing restaurant operations when someone with less experience or expertise had for whatever reason become overwhelmed and was failing to meet his personal goals and upper management's financial goals.

In most cases a high-powered general manager can go into a situation like I mentioned and have an immediate impact on the business. Sometimes he can't. This is especially true when supervision's perception of what is actually wrong is distorted.

Ultimately, supervisors are responsible for the success of each restaurant they oversee. A weak or insecure supervisor will sometimes embellish, mislead, or misdirect information in order to put the blame on the manager and take the heat off of himself for the moment. Unless the next level of management is on top of their game, a simple problem turns into a fiasco.

I must confess I am writing this from a very different perspective now than when I was taking action eleven years ago to relocate to Albuquerque.

Knowledge and experience are invaluable teachers. If I had known then what I know now, I would have opted for more information.

We sold the house in Copperas Cove, packed our stuff, and headed west. Misty and her husband's family had decided to move to the East Coast. Tonya and Justin decided they wanted to live with Kevin Jr. Since Los Alamos was only an hour and half away from Albuquerque, we approved it.

We bought a really cute adobe-looking house on the northwest side of Albuquerque, located in Rio Rancho. It was pretty small but served our purpose.

What we both really cherished about this house was the immaculate, professionally landscaped backyard that included a full-size swimming pool.

A four-and-half-foot tan stucco wall enclosed the backyard area. A seven-foot archway allowed access into a beautiful garden area, which was also protected by similar stucco walls. The covered patio area just off the pool was engulfed with vine foliage that in the summer covered not only the patio but almost the entire back of the house. Shrub and flowerbeds were plentiful.

On the opposite side of the pool was a very large area of bluegrass that was protected from the New Mexico midday sun by two very large ponderosa pine trees.

My favorite times of the day to enjoy this quiet space were early in the morning or late in the afternoon. It was my sanctuary.

Chapter 5
Set Up for Success or Failure?

As I mentioned in the previous chapter, sometimes a high-powered general manager can fix situations and other times it is impossible. It did not take me long to assess the situation as not only improbable but next to impossible to fix at this location.

Operationally, there were many concerns and issues. Those kind of opportunities are easily addressed and overcome. The trick is to get your staff to buy into what is missing and set new exciting expectations.

In order to accomplish this, a manager must play the cards he is dealt and develop a bond of trust between the staff and himself. The best way I know of to do this is to come in soft and observe what is really going on. I like to talk to everyone and seek their feedback. I have to know without a doubt what they need, want, and expect from me, before I ask for their loyalty and long-term commitment.

The management cards I was dealt came from a pretty ugly deck. My immediate area supervisor was insecure in his position. My first assistant manager was burned out because in the past fifteen months she had seen three previous general managers get terminated. My second assistant manager had a very serious drinking problem.

During my first week at this location, I caught my only crew leader stealing money, which promptly ended her career. Additionally, John Willingham's sixteen- and seventeen-year-old daughters were working at this restaurant.

There was no doubt that this location was going to test my patience.

Although the people issues are always a concern, they can be resolved, redesigned, and reenergized. And although this management team was not accomplishing its goals, the actual problem holding this store back was a change in the market location. If a restaurant location has become bad because the marketplace has shifted, there is not anything a general manager can do to fix it.

Over a period of time, I brought this to the attention of my area supervisor, who failed to take the information up the chain of command, so I finally tired of the situation and predicted another restaurant closing in my letter of resignation to John Willingham. A year and half later, this location was closed and sold.

Chapter 6
Neo-Tech Man

About the same time I left the restaurant management company, I received in the mail a manuscript entitled *Neo-Tech Discovery*. To this day I have no idea who sent this information to me because there was no return address.

I opened up the container and pulled out the rather lengthy manuscript. I began flipping through the pages and realized the information was formatted more like a manual than a manuscript.

Within the document was what the author referred to as 114 neo-tech advantages that, when mastered, would form a matrix of knowledge so well crafted that prosperity, power, and romantic love would be forever at your fingertips.

The directions were simple: "read all the advantages in order, make no prejudgments, do your own thinking, and forget judgments made by others."

Another intriguing statement that neo-tech makes is that if you are employed by the government, a lawyer, a preacher, or a neo cheater of any fashion, the information contained in the *Neo-Tech Discovery* manuscript cannot be made available to you under any circumstances. I found that statement to be not only very bold but fascinating as well.

I spent the next three months inhaling and digesting the ideas and concepts previously noted as the neo-tech advantages. I discovered it to be very difficult for me to embrace the entire 114 principles during that three months of exploration. I experienced a ton of emotional upheaval as I began to question many of the belief systems that I had firmly put in place over my lifetime. It was a challenge to look at these systems with fresh eyes and realize that what I was hanging on to was no longer serving me.

My journey with neo-tech lasted three years before I was able to totally comprehend and apply all the principles. All I can tell you is the information contained in the manuscript developed into a very powerful matrix and when I realized, understood, practiced, initiated, and put it into action, I was able to accomplish anything I needed within the business community that I chose.

Most of the time an opponent did not even realize that what was occurring was actually what was supposed to and was in his or her best interest all along.

Since I do not know who will be reading this information, the only things I can say about becoming a neo-tech master is that the information I received enhanced my ability to see beyond what the average person is able to see within himself and others. It is a selfless existence that on the surface appears to many as being self-centered. It was the beginning of knowing my personal power and always using my authority instead of my position of power when dealing with people, in order to achieve a desired result.

The Aristotelian principles I mastered proved to be invaluable tools that opened doors and yet protected me from all adversity. People who attempted to threaten, intimidate, or coerce me realized quickly that my self-esteem, production of competitive values, and competitive results would neutralize them.

And although there were many principles about God, mystics, and the nature of man that I could not agree with, I was able to adjust and slice through those principles and come away with an awakening of my true self-awareness, and in reality nurture and enhance my relationship with the Almighty.

Prior to neo-tech I really believed I was a giver. I did a lot of things for people. I bought stuff for needy people; I gave what I thought was helpful advice to people I cared about, and I invested my time and money in people whom I believed needed and wanted a second chance in life. Here is an example.

In 1988, my two best cooks came to me with a business idea they believed would give them their second chance. I listened to them, investigated their concept, and decided to invest in them 5,000 dollars to help them get started. They agreed to continue working at the restaurant full time until the other business was profitable enough to support them. They also agreed that before they left my employment they would train their replacements.

I had my accountant set up a limited liability company with me owning 51 percent and my cooks owning (through sweat equity) 49 percent of the company. In addition the company would pay back the initial money used to fund the project at an interest rate of 7 percent over a thirty-six-month period of time. At the end of three years, I would sell all my interest in the company back to my cooks based upon five times the earnings. The day after all the paperwork was finalized, I funded the project. The day after that, neither of them showed up to work. I went by the house they were renting and it was cleaned out. They were gone and so was the 5000 dollars!

At first I was really mad at myself and very disappointed in them. I was actually more angry that I had lost my two best cooks than I was about losing the money. I knew I could replace the money over time, but I needed my cooks now. I just couldn't figure out why this happened. Six months would pass before I would understand.

My restaurant was on the far west side of Fort Worth and I had just come out of a meeting on the far east side of Fort Worth. I decided to stop at a mom-and-pop burger joint to grab some lunch. They didn't have a drive-thru, so I had to go inside. As I walked through the front door, guess who I saw in the kitchen making burgers. Oh yeah, it's true. When my ex-cook looked up, our eyes met. His eyes quickly filled with what could best be described as terror.

I sat down with my back to the kitchen. When the waitress came, I ordered a cheeseburger, fries, and a Coke. About halfway through my meal, my old best cook asked if he could sit down and talk. I, of course, obliged him.

He told me that he and my other cook had never seen that much money in one lump sum before and they sort of just lost their minds. They figured I had put a contract out on them so they had gone underground, living in one flophouse after another until the money ran out. I listened intensely as he recanted their plight. When he finished I had the impression he was waiting on me to demand that he and my other cook pay me back the 5,000. Instead, I told him that stealing my money actually robbed them of their future and stole away their second chance. I explained to him the money was never as important to me as they were. I apologized to him for making what seemed to me a simple business deal, that appeared to them a complicated bunch of legalese, which resulted in them doubting their ability to become successful. I told him the idea that I might have put a contract out on them was a pretty bizarre thought.

He stated my military background freaked them out and they knew that if I wanted to find them I would. I agreed with his assumption but I softened the impact by explaining to him I had no intention of doing anybody harm.

I felt they had punished themselves enough. I finished my lunch, wished him well, and left the restaurant feeling very good. I couldn't figure out why I felt so good. But from that day forward, I have always remembered that feeling of blissful goodness. I just couldn't understand why forgiving these guys for stealing my money made me feel so good.

The true reality of the above story was in forgiving these guys for taking advantage of our situation. It was a form of giving without expecting anything in return. Basically I let them off the hook. A real giver is able to give freely because it makes him feel good to give. A true giver doesn't make silent contracts or expect anything in return for the gift he is giving. To do so takes away the joy a giver feels. Although I didn't realize it, what I was feeling was real joy.

As sad as this sounds, I missed out on this feeling of joy most of my life because of the silent contracts I made and the things I would expect from the people I was giving to. My belief system was "Nothing is free", so if I am willing to give you something, it should be okay for me to expect something in return.

I remember being a ten-year-old child and the preacher talking about tithing. It seemed like every Sunday he would say, "If you give ten percent of your income to the church, God will bless you."

I was just a kid with a Sunday paper route that would net me about five dollars a week. When the offering plate was passed to me, I would grudgingly put in my fifty-cent piece and then wait impatiently for my blessing. This routine continued until I went off to college. I was thankful for many things, but I never figured out what the preacher meant by God giving faithful givers blessings.

I now understand what I had failed to hear and comprehend years ago was the state of mind to be in when you are giving to another. The Bible tells us to give with a cheerful heart. Since the human heart is greatly influenced by the human mind, the thought of being cheerful when giving is the platform from which the blessing is launched. With your mind and heart aligned, you are now ready to receive the blessing God has promised. The blessing is simple but has a powerful, long-lasting effect on the human psyche. When you experience this blessing, the feeling becomes almost addictive. The English word "joy" contains an influx of special energy that does not accurately describe its life-changing capabilities. The energy you receive in giving without expecting anything in return is a feeling that is returned to you tenfold in the form of blissful joy.

Prior to my discovery of neo-tech, I was in reality a taker disguised as a giver. Understanding this simple idea helped me uncover and rediscover real joy in my life.

When you begin to investigate your inner thoughts, you may come to the conclusion that you no longer feel the need for greed. When you awaken to the joy of giving and forgiving without expecting anything in return, the human dilemmas you face will improve daily. Creating situations where everyone involved comes out a winner will be a natural occurrence for you.

Your ability to resolve concerns or issues will become a simple process.

So let us assume you are a taker disguised as a giver and you feel the need to change. What steps can you take to incorporate this new way of thinking?

Step 1: Be of service to others. You don't have to be in charge of people to be of service to them. For example, allow a person who is in a hurry to cut in front of you in the grocery store or at the bank.

Step 2: Beware of how you respond, react, and interact with people. Train yourself to control your response to a person's negative comments about you, or directly toward you, through listening closely to what is being said. Determine whether this information is on target and useful. If the comments are truthful, be prepared to take action to change. If the comments are not true and are not of any value to you, be prepared to forgive the person who made the comments and turn the other cheek. Please do not allow your ego to entrap you, making you believe you should retaliate. Instead let the negative energy flow around you and not through you. Be ready to always react in a positive way to a positive person or situation without taking personal advantage of the person or the situation. Sometimes your ego will kick in and the need for greed will open a door that you may want to walk through but don't. Instead allow the positive energy to flow through you and not around you. Enjoy the moment. It will last a lifetime.

Step 3: This final step is critical if you are in a leadership position within the family, business, or teaching communities. No matter what your relationship is to another human being, whether this person wants to put you on a pedestal or chooses to persecute you, your response toward him must be in the form of unconditional love. This is not an easy concept to learn, much less accomplish, when someone is being hateful to you.

Learning to master these ideas will allow you to find balance. If you allow your ego to get inflated when being praised, you will get too high. If you allow your ego to get deflated when being reprimanded, you will get too low. When you learn to control your ego, you will be on your way to finding real joy in your life, while at the same time you will eliminate most of the negative belief systems you have naturally created, for what you have believed was for the purpose of your protection. You too will discover that those belief systems no longer serve you and therefore are of no value. One by one they will be dissolved, forgotten, and naturally replaced as you awaken (and you will) to a new and more productive way of viewing you, the people you love, and the world in which you reside.

CHAPTER 7
Unexpected Surprises

Sometimes unexpected surprises are welcome and a lot of fun. Sometimes unexpected surprises provide you with a dose of reality or a wake-up call.

It had been two months since I had left the restaurant management company and I was still unemployed. I wish I could tell you it was because I was being very selective. The truth be known, I was unexpectedly surprised when I was continuously told by the restaurant human resource folks with whom I interviewed that they would give me a call, but they didn't. Granted, my resume made me look a little flaky, but I figured in a face-to-face interview I could explain in a satisfactory way what the heck had been going on. The human resource departments were not buying it. I kept thinking that if only I could talk with a restaurant supervisor or a director, I could get them to see the value in hiring me. It didn't take long and my thoughts became reality.

Out of the blue I received another unexpected surprise. Bobby Merritt called. After our conversation I thought it was so strange that this had happened at this particular time in my life, when all the doors and windows to all the restaurant organizations I had applied with were not only closed but nailed down tightly.

I now had the opportunity to discuss a career move with a restaurant owner.—not a supervisor or director but an *owner*.

Before Bobby's phone call I had even contemplated leaving the restaurant industry. Frankly, even though I loved the business, I started to doubt whether managing restaurants and I were a good fit. I decided to try and figure out why on one hand I loved this business, while on the other hand I also disdained it. So one night I sat down at the dining room table, whipped out a piece of paper, and began to do some soul searching. What I came up with didn't surprise or enlighten me, but I will share this information with you anyway, just in case there are other restaurant folks reading this who maybe questioning their own ability to lead others.

One of the reasons I loved this business so much was because I had become an adrenal junky. I was at my peak performance during rush periods. I thrived under pressure in an attempt to ensure every guest got his or her food in a fast, friendly, and helpful manner.

I also received a tremendous amount of satisfaction teaching, coaching, and mentoring my staff. Nothing to me was more rewarding than molding a solid, productive management team that could execute the business while they simultaneously showed genuine appreciation for the folks they were responsible for.

Another perk for me was hiring a young person who had never worked outside his parents' home before, this being his first job, oh my! Most of us who work in the restaurant industry realize the huge responsibility that we have in ensuring this young person's experience is a rewarding one.

What I disdained the most about the restaurant industry was its innate ability to suffocate great leadership. The strength of the industry is also its Achilles heal. The attitude throughout the industry is wanting really strong general managers but then thinking they need to baby sit them with up-close, personal, in-your-face supervision.

In reality, if a supervisor or area manager (a term in some organizations that denotes a person with multiple store responsibility) spends enough quality time coaching, mentoring, and teaching a general manager in what constitutes great leadership, he at some point should be able to move into more of a consultant's role. When this occurs, the relationship between the general manager and the area supervisor dramatically improves and that relationship becomes enabled. Everyone involved feels mutual respect, productivity is handsomely improved, and general manager turnover becomes nil. This attitude also filters throughout the restaurant, creating an environment that is heroic in nature.

On the other hand, when an area supervisor or area manager's (a term I distain) role is reduced to being an information-giver from the top, an auditor, or just a plain old watchdog, the best general managers will go elsewhere. In this kind of environment, everyone involved is concerned with covering up their mistakes instead of being focused on improving their results. People should be learning from their mistakes and not wasting time believing they have to cover them up or by making excuses for why they happened in the first place. When people feel threatened or intimidated, their productivity is vastly diminished. What I disdained was an environment where time was being wasted, crippling people's ability to lead and diminishing their god-given genius.

I realized my love for this business was honorable and my disdain for the business was not. So I set my mind to mentor vertically, meaning I would share my insights with my boss no matter how painful for him or how difficult I would appear to be to deal with.

Bobby wound up offering me a position. He had opened a door—the only door that was available for me to walk through, if I chose to. My decision to go through that door or not go through that door was based solely in Bobby's eyes the day I was fired in Florida. I had known from that day forward that Bobby Merritt was a man of great honor—a man whom I felt in my heart center was fair and just. What he was willing to offer me was an opportunity. What I did with that opportunity was going to be totally up to me. I decided to seize his opportunity and walked boldly into the unknown, determined to be flexible to change and willing to compromise. I am sorry to say that my determination failed to last but one week.

I was immediately challenged by my supervisor, regional director, and the director of operations. Compromise and flexibility went out the window, which created just a little chaos. Bobby intervened and calmed the waters. It took from October 31, 1995 until the end of March, 1996 to gain just a little respect from these old-time operators. By the end of August 1996, they began to see some genius behind my methods, which I am certain appeared at first as madness to them. I will always be thankful they gave me enough space to try the things I wanted to try. Their reward was double-digit sales increases and the doubling of store profits the first year.

The second-year results were much the same. I can't say there were not any bumps along the way, because there were. I spent a great deal of time thinking outside the lines, which is sometimes not totally appreciated. Outside-the-box thinking sometimes comes across as being dissatisfied, when in truth all I was doing was questioning the many "sacred cows" that could have been put to sleep and then ground into hamburger meat.

All organizations have sacred cows, but most organizations don't like to discuss them. It is very obvious when you find one, because the argument that is used to protect a sacred cow from slaughter is always the same: "we have always done it this way." That comment to me is as irritating as the statement; "It's not my job." Both comments will cause me to question not only your integrity but intelligence as well. Anyway, I agree with the book *Sacred Cow's Make the Best Burgers*.

As you continue this journey with me, you too will learn that the significant people and sacred cows that show up crossing your path do so for reasons you may not be aware of. It is my understanding they are brought to us to assist in helping us learn lessons we are here to learn. They may also appear as pathfinders and opportunities when we have lost our sense of direction.

It is obvious to me now that Bobby was sent to me as my pathfinder and his entire upper management team came along to teach me lessons I needed to learn. What is really very cool about all of this is the underlying lessons I was able to teach them too After all, life should be a very busy two-way street.

At this point in my story, I must stop and tell you a "sub-story." Some of you may think this sub-story is somewhat irreverent; however, it is a testimony to my continued search for my own personal growth and spiritual awakening. I feel the need to share it with you. Besides, everyone enjoys a good story.

In the spring of 1996, I noticed our happy-hour sales between 2:00 p.m. and 5:00 p.m. were not as strong as the rest of the market. Typically what is done to help drive sales is implementing some form of local store marketing. I have never been a big believer in discounting. In fact, I asked Mickey Miller (my area supervisor) in December of 1995 if I could stop happy hour in January.

Happy-hour consisted of giving someone two drinks for the price of one. He explained to me this was not only a Merritt-wide policy, but SONIC Industries supported this policy as well. I countered this idea by explaining I was certain I could actually execute my restaurant better during happy hour with less people and lower my food and paper costs at the same time. I assured him we would honor happy-hour discounts in the month of January and February if the guests requested the discount.

I must interject there were actually two kinds of happy-hour discounting in place at this time. For one form of happy hour, if a guest bought one drink we would give them a second drink for free. This made very little sense to me, because many of my guest's were by themselves and didn't want the second drink. This meant we were dumping a lot of drinks down the drain.

The other form of discounting was selling a drink for half price. This made more sense to me, but it was hard for me to swallow the idea I was giving away 50 percent of the most profitable item on the menu while it cost me more labor to do so. I felt happy hour was a sacred cow that needed killing.

Mickey listened intently while I went over my reasons for not wanting to be a team player. After I had finished, he surprised me and gave me permission to stop happy hour. He also warned me that my sales would be affected. I responded by assuring him that I would be able to improve my costs enough to help offset sales until the sales began to rebound.

Allowing me to do this was a real risk for both of us, because Bobby and the boys (the old-timers who had learned how to build really big happy-hour day parts) would not be very happy about this decision.

The other risk was that if my restaurant didn't execute this change in a very professional way, the other nine partners in the Albuquerque market could suffer too by confusing our happy-hour guests, who did wander from one location to another.

As predicted, my food, paper, and labor costs dropped a little and so did my sales. As I previously mentioned, by early spring our happy-hour day part was still trending below the market average. I thought and thought about what I could do to entice my guests to come see us without having to give the store profits away by discounting.

The idea, although truly unconventional, came to me around three o'clock one morning. I woke up long enough to write down two words: *thought energy*. I awoke around 6:00 a.m. and read what I had written down. I shrugged it off, showered, shaved, and dressed for work. As I was standing in front of the mirror, tying my tie, I realized what the two words meant. It was the seed the cabdriver had planted almost sixteen years ago, which had apparently grown roots over the many years and was now perhaps ready to sprout.

His words came rushing back to me like he was right there whispering them to me; "The same energy that grows your hair and fingernails is also contained in pictures, music, and *your thoughts*. Vibration patterns are different, but it is the same energy. Human thoughts are just fast-moving energy. When manifesting thought energy, it must be good for everyone. You must learn to connect your physical self with your higher self. Manifesting thought energy was like a prayer on steroids, supercharged."

I then remembered the most important phrase he used: "when you learn to do this, trust in it—and *you will*—you will live each and every day from that day forward in amazement."

As I finished tying my tie I looked at my reflection in the mirror. Suddenly, an astounding feeling came over me. I leaned on the dresser, looking directly into my own eyes, and said aloud, "Why me?" "And how did the cabdriver know sixteen years earlier I would even attempt to try, much less be able, to learn this?"

I got weak in the knees and lost my breath for a moment. I knew enough by now that if I did not believe I could manifest and then project my thought energy, my faith would be weakened by my unbelief and would automatically shut down the channel between my physical self and my higher self.

I decided that day to try to influence people driving by my restaurant to instead stop in and give us the opportunity to provide them with a wow experience. (A wow experience is far exceeding the guest's expectation.)

It did not take me long to realize the cabdriver had at his disposal a lot more energy to spare than I could even muster. All he did was close his eyes and within fifteen seconds his energy was manifested. When I did what he did, all that happened was my head immediately filled with thoughts I couldn't find a way to control. This occurred every day. It was obvious to me I must be missing something.

A couple of weeks later, I was in the back storage area straightening up the stockroom and an idea popped into my head. *Maybe I just need to sit and become very still so I can focus all my attention on visualizing what I would like to project,* I thought. So for forty-five minutes I sat there and visualized juicy hamburgers, plump foot-long hotdogs, ice-cold cherry limeades, golden crisp french fries, and fresh, hot onion rings. As those thoughts came into my head, I would then toss them out onto the street in front of the restaurant.

When I finally stood up to walk back to the front of the restaurant, I noticed I felt unusually tired. I also noticed we appeared to be busier than usual. I decided I should run an hourly report that would either confirm or deny this impression I was getting. I remember this queasy feeling I had in the pit of my stomach as the report was printing. *What if this stuff really works? What if I really have the power to influence people's thoughts? Have I somehow crossed over the line of common reasoning?*

The report finish printing and as I looked at it, I gasped out loud. "Oh my!" During the time I was in a state of meditation, we had run 25 percent more sales than we were used to and the sales were continuing to come in at the same pace.

I got into a line position in order to assist the flow of food. I looked over at my wife and she was grinning at me. I wondered if she somehow knew what was happening, and more importantly, why it was happening, I was not ready to share this information with her or anyone else at this point. Maybe, just maybe, this occurrence was just a coincidence. Again, one of the cabdriver's statements came into mind. "I see we have a doubting Thomas to deal with." I also realized he had said, *we* and not *I*. I contemplated who else he was referring to.

The next day I went through the entire process again—ya know, just to satisfy my curiosity. The results were the same. It seemed whatever I was thinking and then projecting, we wound up selling. People even quit asking for happy-hour discounts.

I made it a habit to disappear every day around the same time, under the pretext of needing some quiet time. I also became aware the staff was starting to question why it seemed I was a little scatterbrained when I came back from my quiet time. I too wondered why this process was so physically demanding on me. I always felt so exhausted after each session that all I wanted to do was get away and rest my mind. It didn't take long before the answer was revealed to me.

When going through this process, I had to use all my stored-up physical energy in order to project my manifested thoughts. I didn't know it then, but there was a simpler, more economical way to do this. It would take some years and a lot of trial and error to understand this process.

I am not a liberty to share sales numbers with you, but it didn't take but a couple of weeks of daily meditation before Mickey Miller was in my store predicting my month-end sales for March, which even I thought were outrageous. By the end of the month we had even surpassed his estimates.

The volume was growing now in all the day parts. It grew so quickly it out grew my staff. We had gone from being slightly bored to being overwhelmed in just one month. I needed more good people and I needed them now. My focus moved from store sales to finding more good people I could hire. I was amazed when folks from nowhere started to show up looking for work.

By the end of April, 1996, my store was staffed with more talented, highly motivated, and well-trained employees than I ever dreamed possible in such a short period of time.

For the next two years, I dedicated myself to insuring these folks were protected and well taken care of. We had a lot of fun and many cherished moments that will be with each of us always.

I must add a footnote here. Over the next ten years, I would very carefully choose with whom I shared my newly discovered ability to influence sales and drive profits.

Using neo-tech principles and learning how to manifest my thoughts, I moved quickly into upper management, providing the opportunity for me to have an even greater impact on the lives of those I became responsible for.

I also understood how important it was to give thanks and credit where it was due. I learned it was actually more rewarding and fun to remain in the background, applauding my folks' success, than having the need to be center stage.

In March, 1998, I received an opportunity to take a promotion to co-supervisor in the Farmington, New Mexico market, under the guidance of Ted Sprinkle. Over the past two and half years, Ted, his wife Sherry, Cindy, and I had become very good friends. I felt I could take some pressure off of Ted and help impact his market in a very positive way. I also knew that if I got myself in trouble, Ted would be there to bail me out.

Although it was very difficult for Cindy and I to leave our wonderful team behind, our hope was they would all be fine. We said our tearful goodbyes and left for Farmington.

Chapter 8
Coincidence or Certainty?

The sun was just coming up as I stood on my third-story deck overlooking the glade. It was late May, 1998. The air was cool, crisp, and clean-smelling.

Cindy came out with her faithful cup of coffee in her hand and we stood there arm in arm, enjoying the moment.

I have always been fascinated with sunrises and sunsets. In Farmington, New Mexico it is very difficult to determine which provides the onlooker with a more exhilarating experience. They are such an inspiration to observe. I can't think of a better way to start or end a day.

When the sun had cleared the horizon and was fully visible, I turned to Cindy and said, "Isn't it strange. Here we are back in Farmington again."

Cindy seemed lost in her own thoughts but responded with one of her great smiles and replied, "Strange in what way?"

"Well, we left here in March of 1992 and came back almost six years to the day. Don't you think that is just a little too coincidental? I mean, over the past thirty days I have been wondering if perhaps Farmington was where we were supposed to be all along."

Surefooted, she retorted, "That would have meant we would have missed out on all that fun we had, remember?"

This time she was grinning and I laughed out loud. "Yeah, I remember all that fun we've had! Someday I will write a book about all the fun we've had the last six years."

Tenderly she said, "Hey, I agree! Maybe there is a reason why we have come full circle. I also realize the past six years have not been easy on you, the family, or myself, but here we are again. If there is a purpose behind all this, it will be revealed."

"I know you're right, but if we were supposed to stay in Farmington and I led us on this wild goose chase, I would just like to know why," I wondered aloud.

She smiled again, replying in a teasing way, "Didn't you just tell me you needed material for your book, silly!"

"Okay, I have had enough abuse for one day," I stated jokingly. Thinking out loud, I said, "Maybe I am making too much of this, but it just seems really strange to me that we are back in Farmington again. Anyway, I have to head up to Durango, Colorado. I will be back in time to share tonight's sunset with you," I stated lovingly. I pulled her close and gave her gentle hug.

She responded with a long, wet, tender kiss and said, "I will be waiting!"

Still holding her, I gazed into her deep brown eyes. In that fleeting moment I realized how lucky I was to have this woman in my life. She was the one person in my world who had always believed in me. I was certain in that instant that we, for some reason, were back here for a purpose. It wasn't coincidental.

Chapter 9
The Land of Entrapment

New Mexico is known throughout the entire Southwest as the Land of Enchantment. It is the state slogan. Some folks living in New Mexico refer to the slogan as the Land of Entrapment, the reason being once you are living there; it is very hard to leave so much loveliness behind.

New Mexico is rich in history and natural rustic beauty. From Las Cruces to Albuquerque, to Santa Fe, to Gallup, to the Four Corners you will find high deserts, mountains, rock formations, lakes, and streams that will dazzle your senses. Beware: the Land of Enchantment will awaken the child within you.

Certain areas of New Mexico are also steeped in some unexplainable phenomena. For instance, I have been told that in the Four Corners area, between Shiprock and Farmington, there is a very powerful energy source that comes directly out of the ground. This has never been scientifically proven; however, some of the elder Navajo Indians believe this energy has a direct impact on the weather in the Four Corners. After living in Farmington for over four years, I can attest to the weather being very seldom harsh and nearly perfect. The weather is only one aspect that appears hard to explain.

I have also been told that people who struggle with headaches have a difficult time living in or around the Four Corners area. The mystics believe the additional energy coming out of the ground is just too much for some people to absorb.

The Navajo Nation appears poor economically, but a very little-known fact is there are more millionaires per capita located in Gallup, New Mexico than anywhere else in the country. If it were not for the Navajo Nation, Farmington, Gallup, and Shiprock would struggle economically.

The younger generations of Navajos are also becoming big-time players within the work force, while the elders within the nation are still cloaked in very powerful mysticism and tradition. The most successful young Navajos are able to find a balance between both fractions. Several of my partner/managers in Gallup, Shiprock, and Farmington supported their traditions and restaurants in a remarkable way. Ted Sprinkle had done a fantastic job building mutually powerful relationships with all these young entrepreneurs. My goal was to continue to enhance those relationships by developing a bond based on my respect and my admiration of this market's many accomplishments.

Ted was considered Mr. SONIC in the Four Corners. His reputation was known and highly respected far and wide. His wife, Sherry, although very supportive of Ted's career with SONIC, was also very involved with the community. Individually they complimented each other nicely, but together they were an unstoppable force of energy to reckon with.

No matter how involved they were in projects, they always found the time to share their knowledge and experiences with Cindy and me. They had a unique way of getting information to us in a variety of settings that were fun, interesting, and challenging, especially for me. They had set the stage. All we did was take their helpful information, put a little spin on it, and apply it by taking action.

Ted turned his responsibility for daily store operations over to me so he could focus all his attention on searching for new locations and building new stores. He would also be the one who made the decisions on when to purchase equipment for existing locations.

I had no interest in becoming the new "Mr. SONIC." Ted was an expert at rubbing shoulders and making people around him feel good. I was contented to remain a quiet force in the background of daily occurrences. I was able to do this only because Ted empowered me to do so. I had his complete trust and authority to make the decisions necessary in order to help our partners accomplish their personal and financial goals. With this kind of environment and flexibility, I was able to perform my responsibilities with clarity and purpose.

The implementation of Aristotelian principles forged a solid platform from which immediate positive results translated into less turnover and better productivity. The concept of building powerful inner circles within each restaurant was met with very little resistance. Because of this, most of the management teams began to execute their restaurants at a higher state of consistency and efficiency. In becoming aware that *their* people were *their* most important resource, the partner/managers began to rethink their position on the importance of creating work environments that made it possible for almost anyone who tried and wanted to be successful and happy to succeed in doing so.

I focused all my time and energy building relationships with each of my individual teams. I did not want anyone to fear my presence when I was in their restaurants. My intent was to get the people I was responsible for to relax and be able to enjoy themselves whenever I was able to be with them.

I needed to find out truthfully how I could best serve them. I wanted to know what their goals and dreams were. I also wanted to observe them in action without them feeling like they were being observed. I always looked for what they were doing right so I would have the opportunity to tell them how proud I was that *they* had decided to come to work for SONIC. I also wanted them to know how much I personally appreciated all their hard work and dedication to our organization.

It did not surprise me when the morale of the market started to go through the roof. Were we perfect operationally? No! Were we better operationally today than we were yesterday? Yes!

When you understand the hidden meaning behind the act of becoming noble, you will begin to restructure your internal map of reality. The secret is, although you possess many outstanding qualities, those qualities do not make you better than anyone else. They just provide you with the opportunity to become better than you were yesterday. This hidden secret is the key to understanding your true nobility. It is your human birthright and a privilege to understand that trying to be better than another person only causes that person who is competing to be filled with false feelings of limited satisfaction or daily feelings of failure.

Famous athletes, great leaders, creative inventors, or any other person who naturally creates competition doesn't waste much energy worrying about those who will want to compete against them. They instead are totally absorbed in what they can do to improve themselves on a day-to-day basis.

If you are bound and determined to compete instead of cooperate, compete within yourself but cooperate outside yourself. Trying to be better than you were yesterday is a noble task. I promise you won't be disappointed if this is your desired motivation. It is your choice, of course, in learning to be happy within yourself.

Chapter 10
The Golden Boy

The one lesson I learned very early on in my restaurant career was that without great people who were dedicated and loyal to the organization, I became a very average leader. Knowing this, my first and foremost concern was to instill these energies in everyone who worked with me. There is no magic in knowing this. The magic occurs when everyone understands how important they are to the success of everyone else involved. When everyone is attempting to be better than they were the day before, is the instant greatness is born.

It would be like watching a ballet or seeing a fast ground ball coming at you so slowly you can see the seams of the ball turning in slow motion. At that moment in space and time, you come to the realization that your focus and vision have clearly inspired the sum of all parts toward greatness. Although greatness can be in your grasp one moment and gone the next, it can also be developed and nurtured. When a leader really believes, understands, and puts into action the powerful energies of understanding, patience, loving discipline, appreciation, and reverent honesty, he will influence and inspire greatness in the lives of the people he is responsible for. It is so simple it eludes most of us.

I also realized that my personal success would be in direct proportion to the success my folks were having. I knew if I invested all my time and energy teaching, coaching, mentoring, and sharing most of my knowledge with the leadership in the market, the results would be lucrative for all concerned. In addition, I also used my honed ability to project my manifested thought energy to assist in driving sales. The results were astounding.

The chief financial officer for the Merritt Group, Leslie Berryman, labeled me "the golden boy" because it seemed wherever I went, whatever I touched turned to gold.

From an ego standpoint, Leslie's label was very flattering, especially since it came from her. Of all the CFOs I have known over the past twenty years, I hold Ms. Berryman in the highest regard. Her knowledge, business savvy, and ability to communicate honestly and fairly is well known and respected throughout the industry. To say she is one of Bobby's key assets is to actually diminish the important role she plays in his success.

I wanted to share this tidbit about being called "the golden boy" only to give me the opportunity to give credit where it was actually due. Although I had many untested insights, ideas, and concepts regarding leading people, the partners were the ones who were instrumental in taking this information and applying the principles. Without their genius, steadfastness, and willingness to forge ahead into unknown territory, my reputation as "the golden boy" could very easily have become "the one-store-wonder boy" whose insights, ideas, and concepts didn't work for anyone but him.

If any of my ex-partners in the Farmington Market get a chance to read this book, my genuine outlook for each of you is for your continued success and personal happiness. I will always be thankful and appreciative each of you were in place before my arrival in Farmington. I think about each of you as time passes, feeling certain our lives crossed at just the right moment in time. I thank each of you for assisting in my growth in learning how to lead you. God bless all of you collectively and each of you and your families individually. Please know you and your families are missed and loved unconditionally.

Chapter 11
Open Your Mind, Attaching It to No-Thing

My intention when writing the first ten chapters of this book was an attempt to introduce you to me. From the "Introduction" to "The Golden Boy," I wanted to bring you along on the nineteen-year journey that actually climaxes in January 2006.

My hope in writing this story is that although the content may be different than what is contained in your own personal story, perhaps we share some of the same struggles and difficulties. Although the characters are different, perhaps the relationships we share are similar but have had very different outcomes. I don't know what your purpose is for reading this book other than that you are aware by now that you have been living by your five senses, driven by your ego/personality, and frankly, you know by the many hints I have been giving you that there is a better, more productive way to live your life.

I have entitled this chapter, "Open Your Mind and Attach It to No-Thing" to assist you in enabling your human mind to be readily prepared to at least read the next two chapters with an open mind. If you enter into the next two segments of this story with a closed mind, you will be skeptical, judgmental, and uncomfortable. So, with that said, open your mind and replace your attachment to being judgmental and skeptical with optimism, seeking out your own unbiased personal truths.

In April, 1999, Sherry Sprinkle had arranged for a reader, Ja-Zon, to perform a tarot reading for me. It was her birthday present to me. Sherry was a big believer in the metaphysical world, so it was not surprising to me she would spring this on me. Besides, we had had many opportunities to discuss our very different points of view pertaining to the many kinds of religious dogma available throughout the world, the different interpretations of the Bible, and of course my steadfast, Jesus the Christ.

And although I cannot recite any particular conversations we had, I do remember the tone and attitude of those lively conversations. Sherry was an excellent listener—very patient, understanding, and unobtrusive. Her eyes were soft while at the same time penetrating. She smiled often while I was talking, never taking offense to my point of view.

When she spoke it was in a state of calmness. She was specific and clear in her perspective. Her words were simple and yet carried a message of assurance so powerful they would pierce my armor over time.

I, on the other hand, realized this woman was lost, and I needed to assist her in finding her own personal salvation. I was an expert at playing the black-and-white game, in which white was my perspective, and therefore white, must always win. Needless to say, I did not listen very well in the beginning, and I was, to say the least, a bit combative. I felt this was okay because I had lived my entire life with a belief system firmly planted in my human mind, which I perceived to be my warrior mentality. In addition, I had always been an extreme competitor. My perspective of competition supported my belief system, which fed my ego/personality and reinforced my conservative point of view.

Basically this meant that if you were silly enough to challenge me in an area of my life in a way that I felt threatened one of my core belief systems, you had better bring your lunch, because I would be super prepared to battle with you. And although the neo-tech advantages softened my stance and removed some of the rough edges, when pushed, I would always appear at least a little combatant. This made people uncomfortable.

In the material world, this kind of attitude is reflected as positive and is respected. No one likes to see another person get pushed around. The person being pushed around is perceived as weak and of little value. The person who is doing the pushing is perceived as a bully.

Up to this point in my life, I had spent a great deal of my time fighting with bullies. Often I would lose, but the bully always knew he had been in a fight. Bullies take on many shapes and sizes. Individuals, corporations, companies, and government agencies are just a few of the bullies I have battled with.

Although my dealings and discussions with Sherry challenged many of my core beliefs, causing me to react in a combatant way, her response never caused conflict. It was very difficult to fight with someone who was ego-free and responded to an aggressor with love, honor, and an understanding that is deeper than an ocean. It is like shadowboxing. No matter how many punches you throw, you can't make any contact. I had no choice but listen more and question less. Her patience and guiding hand enabled me to begin my process of self-actualization. This would be an attempt to discover my purpose and become the best person I could be. I would be provided a lot of help in a very short period of time because I had lost six years of information when my free will, driven by my ego, chose to leave Farmington the first time in 1992. My birthday present from Sherry would be the beginning of the miracles and the magic that began to show up in my life as I developed faith in knowing I was not and never had been separate from God.

I had seen Ja-Zon at several parties Ted and Sherry had given over the past year. We had never spoken a word to each other prior to our meeting, but I had been encouraged by Sherry in the past to solicit her for a reading. I always said I would but never did. And now Ja-Zon was at my front door.

As a post script, as much as I would like to recant to you our entire conversation, space and time does not warrant the effort. The entire reading was recorded on a tape. I will do my best to highlight the most important information I received that is pertinent at this time.

Ja-Zon was a heavy-set woman with a sweet, angelic face, which did not match her booming alto voice when she spoke. She was very jovial and easy to like. I looked into her bi-speckled eyes and felt peaceful. I was anxious to get started. She pulled out her tarot cards, asking me to shuffle them, just like the lady from India had requested. I did as she requested. She said a very loving prayer asking her guides and God to grant her direction in the reading she was about to give to me. She smiled and began to lay down the cards.

Chapter 12
The Reading

Since I did not request this reading, I posed no questions for Ja-Zon to answer. It was my intent just to sit back, relax, and see what would happen.

Every card Ja-Zon turned over had some significance. As I watched the cards that she turned over, I noticed some were inverted, meaning the picture on the card was upside down. She explained that the meaning of the card would actually be the opposite of what it symbolized because of its inferior position.

As she went through each card one at a time, I realized at some point during the reading that she was giving me information about the life plan I had mapped out for myself prior to my human birth. In conjunction with my life plan, she discussed some of my past lives that her guides/angels felt were pertinent to my understanding the plan I had designed. As bizarre as this whole scenario sounds, the only way she would have known the things she did about me was if she had read this book, which of course would not be written until 2006. As previously mentioned, this reading took place in April of 1999.

Almost immediately after Ja-Zon began the reading, she stated she was sensing a tremendous amount of Celtic and Norseman energy. I told her my ancestors had come over to the United States from Scotland and Denmark.

My father's ancestors had come from Scotland on the Mayflower, and my mother's father had come over from Denmark in the early 1900s. She hesitated for a moment and then responded, stating that would explain the energy she was feeling. She hesitated once again and then began to laugh.

She began again, stating her guides were showing her visuals of a couple of lifetimes I had personally experienced as a Viking. She described me as being physically intimidating and very adept using swords, spears, and axes. She recounted that I had been on the North American continent, but not the states as we know it today. She claimed I had continued to carry the Norseman and Celtic energies with me from those lifetimes to the present lifetime.

She claimed the guides were also showing her I had fought in two of the Crusades. In one lifetime, I had been a knight from Scotland and in another I had been a knight of the Templar's . As a knight of the Templar's I spent most of my time in Jerusalem at the temple of Solomon. Ja-Zon continued, explaining that I had brought knowledge with me from those previous lifetimes that would allow me to see through the illusion of human reality and the injustices thereof. She claimed that as I awakened to this information it would be my choice whether I stayed the course in order to continue making major differences in the lives of many people.

She continued stating that the path I had designed for this lifetime, although difficult, was manageable. I had put in place many lessons that would provide conflict and turmoil in not only my life, but the people I would associate with. This statement had a powerful affect on me. I instantly thought about all the relationships I had been involved with. I could only think of a couple of relationships that had not been fraught with conflict and turmoil.

During this part of the reading, I came to understand I had chosen not to come into this lifetime with the imposing size and physical prowess that had been so beneficial to me in past lifetimes. She said, metaphorically speaking, that I had also decided not to bring my swords with me either. I thought that was ironic because I have quite a collection of knives and swords, as do both my sons. Even though she made it clear this was a metaphor, I wondered if on some level there was a connection, because my fascination with these weapons goes as far back as I can recall.

She stated this was my attempt to see if I could carry over this powerful Celtic and Norseman energy in a much smaller body, in order to use my mind instead of using my unusual physical strength and swordsmanship, as I had in the past, to solve my differences with other people.

In relationship to my mindset; she also wanted to remind me about the warrior's mentality and strong will, which I had crafted, knowing I would have to spend a lot of my time overcoming the obstacles and conflicts that I had set up while designing my life plan. I told her I was very much aware of those personality traits. And even though I had learned to modify them, it was a daily challenge for me to control. She said she understood because my plan was to never take no for an answer. She said this stance in itself would create conflicts but would also lead to many triumphs and successes, interestingly enough, measured by my own standards. We both laughed aloud, knowing on different levels of consciousness this was true.

Smiling, she told me that in the future I should learn to at least look at the other person's side of things—not necessarily to buy into it, but at least be willing to listen and to compromise. She also stated I had been very, very good at being unconventional. Learning to modify that behavior would assist in my life becoming more peaceful.

Ja-Zon also told me I had spent a great deal of personal time over the years reflecting, discovering, and then applying ideas and concepts that in the past, present, and future would continue to bear fruit. She mentioned the energy I carry within always serves me well, in that no matter how bad or good everything around me appeared to be, I always found knowledge in the experience to be thankful for.

She surprised me when she asked if I gave money and other material assets away. I replied that I was very devoted to ensuring that if I became aware someone had a need, I would be there to help. She smiled and said it was now clear what the next card meant. "You do not measure yourself by monetary standards. You measure yourself by your God energy," she responded, adding that these endeavors were not only greatly appreciated and respected in this dimension, but they were also being recognized by the collective consciousness as well. She explained that the collective consciousness was the manifested thought energy that connects us all to one another and to God. I understood her explanation as the universal thoughts of mankind.

The final portion of my reading was a reminder that because I had come into this dimension with knowledge I was carrying over from past lifetimes, I had designed three near-death experiences to ensure I would remember that this human lifetime, which appears as real, is actually an illusion.

She also stated I had put in place three exit points. She explained that because I had come into this lifetime with my eyes wide open, knowing my true nature, this knowledge would cause tremendous conflicts within myself, making life appear to me too tough to deal with from time to time. The exit points were designed as safety nets in case I wanted to cross over. She stated she was very proud of me because when I had come to the third exit point, I almost crossed over but didn't. She said, "Your physical consciousness was willing to give up, but your spiritual consciousness intervened, rearranging the physical world in order to provide relief." She continued, "The physical you connected to the spiritual you, and together they decided that no matter what would occur in the future, the physical you would stay the course." Then she added, "This is very interesting! Confirmation of this will occur in the future and be acknowledged in the physical world to you, by someone very close to you. You will be told the day, month, and year of your physical departure!"

By now I was just a little bit off balance. All this information was floating around in my head while my thoughts kept bumping into one another. Could it actually be possible for one human being to be able to describe in great detail to another human being his past, present, and future endeavors?

I knew I was standing in the middle of a crossroad. A decision had to be made. I could dismiss the information Ja-Zon was giving me, or I could open my heart and mind to its true existence. Could I muster enough faith to believe God and her guides were giving me this information so I could, if I chose to, awaken to my true purpose? And then again, why me?

Before Ja-Zon left my presence, she had one more thing to tell me. With great seriousness in her voice and eyes, she whispered "You have brought a gift with you, and if you choose to share it with others, it will be of great value and very beneficial to many people." Then she chuckled quietly, stating, "This gift possesses a very powerful animal energy." The guides were giving her a vision of a bear. She explained this kind of energy was almost impossible to keep hidden, and when the time was right, I would have a very difficult, if not an impossible, time keeping it a secret.

As she turned to walk out the front door, she looked over her shoulder and said, "You have a lot of work left to do! You need to start listening to your inner voice." She then disappeared around the corner of my house.

I went down to my office, rewound the tape, and listened to the complete reading again and again and again. I finally turned the recorder off and became very still. I pondered and examined the information I had been given. My mind was open to the information I had at my fingertips, but I had too many attachments to be too zealous about Ja-Zon's reading.

Besides, I was a very busy man committed to my own personal goals.

I found that the metaphysical world psychic readers like Ja-Zon live in to be a fascinating place. However, the physical world was still my reality. I put the guidance I had received on hold. If she was right, then my future looked bright! If she was wrong about my future, I might be singing a different song.

Either way, I was okay with it.

Chapter 13
Opportunity knocking

From April, 1999, to February, 2000, everything seemed to happen as I had envisioned and intended. I was quickly approaching my second anniversary as a multi-restaurant supervisor. Sales and profits were expanding well beyond the company average. The morale of the people in the market was of course following that same trend. My personal life could not have been any better.

That was about the time Bobby called offering me what I thought could be the opportunity of a lifetime.

The conversation kind of went like this: "Kevin, its Bobby! Listen, I wanted to tell you what a great job you guys are doing up there in the Farmington."

"Thanks Bob. I appreciate the call and I'll let the folks know you called."

We then proceeded with some small talk, which is always Bobby's way of feeling you out. If he wants to ask you an important question, he zigzags the conversation in order to determine if his timing is correct. Sometimes I think he may just be getting rid of his nervous energy.

So I just sat back and waited. It didn't take long, because Bobby doesn't waste a lot of time.

"Listen, Kev, I've been thinking about opening up the Boise, Idaho market, and I was wondering if you would be interested in moving up there, ya know, to run that market. I mean, do you think you would be up to that kind of challenge?"

Without a moment's hesitation, I clamored, "Bobby, wherever you need me, I'll be there!"

"Can you meet me in Albuquerque next week, and we'll work out the details?"

"Absolutely," I responded. "How about next Tuesday?" he stated clearly.

"Tuesday will be fine, Bob."

"How about I meet you at the Marriot hotel around eleven thirty?"

"Eleven thirty at the Marriot. I'll see you then, and thanks again, Bobby, for the opportunity!"

I got off the phone feeling like I was on cloud nine, and then I came back to earth with a real thud! Here I had told Bobby in so many words we would be willing to move to Boise, Idaho, and I had not even consulted Cindy. What a bozo!

I walked upstairs and found her in the kitchen. Sheepishly I asked, "Guess who I just received a phone call from?"

She stopped what she was doing, turned around, and smiled at me. "Let's see. Do you really expect me to guess? Seriously, I don't have a clue, but I'm certain you are about to tell me," she responded.

I sat down at the dining-room table and motioned her over. Cindy walked over to the table and sat down next to me. "It was Bobby Merritt," I said.

"Really and how is Bobby?" she replied.

"He seemed to be in very good spirits. He is thinking about opening the Boise, Idaho market," I stated.

"Are you kidding?" she responded.

"No, as matter of fact, I am deadly serious," I said.

"Oh my, did he ask you if you were interested in partnering up with him?" she asked emphatically.

"In a manner of speaking, he did," I expounded.

"Well, knowing you like I do, I guess I will start packing!" she stated.

"Whoa, hold on there, sweetie! I did tell him I was interested if the decision was made to move forward, but I have a lot of homework to do before I am certain this is the right move for us," I reported. "On the surface, Boise, Idaho sounds terrific, but the first thing I need to do is get in touch with the chamber of commerce in Boise and get all the data I can. I am supposed to meet with Bobby next Tuesday morning in Albuquerque. I need to get the information from the chamber of commerce overnighted so I have time to look it over and digest it. I must ensure before I meet with Bobby I have as much information at my fingertips as possible," I responded.

She replied, "Do you want me to get in touch with Ja-Zon to see if she can meet with us?"

"Yes, I responded. I think that would be an excellent idea! I'll contact the chamber of commerce, if you will contact Ja-Zon for a reading."

She said she would be more than happy to and then added, "This should certainly give you enough information to make an informed decision, I would think, wouldn't you?"

I quickly reminded her about the last time I had consulted a reader pertaining to the business decision I made in Texas.

She laughed and said, "Oh yes, I remember! But I am certain you will ask enough poignant questions to ensure your decision is based on logic, rather than the one emotional question, Am I going to make a lot of money?" Now we were both laughing.

The next day I received the information from the chamber of commerce. I went down to my office and began going over all the brochures. I had been doing my research for about an hour and a half when Cindy peeked around the corner. "Are you busy?" she asked.

"No, not really, what's up?"

"I just wanted to let you know I spoke with Ja-Zon and she said she could meet with us tomorrow around eleven o'clock in the morning. Are you available?"

"Well, let's see. I have a meeting tomorrow morning at seven thirty. I should be able to wrap that up in a couple of hours, so eleven o'clock should work out just fine."

"Okay, I'll call her back to confirm. I see you received the information from Boise. What do think?"

"So far the demographics look great, and the social economics look very favorable too. To tell you the truth, I'm getting kind of excited about the possibilities. Maybe this afternoon you and I can sit down and go over everything?"

"That would be great. In the meantime I'll call Ja-Zon back, and then I'll fix you something special for lunch!"

I looked up. She was smiling. At that precise moment, I remember thinking how wonderful it was to be married to my very best friend. As she turned to walk away, I also noticed a sparkle in her eye. It was as if she knew something I didn't. I almost asked her what she was thinking but decided not to.

Instead I leaned back in my chair, clasping my hands behind my head, satisfied to just listen to her footsteps as she walked away.

After lunch Cindy and I mulled over the information from the chamber of commerce into the early night, stopping only to answer the phone occasionally and to eat our dinner. After we had finished modeling, compiling, and filing the information, we both felt a sense of relief and were satisfied we had enough information to make a logical decision when the time was appropriate. All we had left to do was to meet with Ja-Zon tomorrow morning and then I would drive to Albuquerque early the following morning to meet with Bobby.

I went to sleep that night and dreamed of all the future possibilities that seemed to be hanging in the balance. I awoke very early that next morning, refreshed, feeling like a kid on Christmas morning. I could hardly wait to unwrap this particular day to see what was going to unfold. I tried to keep my routine as normal as possible, but my thoughts were like lightening and then thunder. One idea after another followed by the question, What if?

On the way to my 7:30 a.m. meeting, I began to settle down and focus my attention on the up coming meeting. I had some interesting information I needed to share with a couple of my partners that I hoped they would find extraordinarily profitable and easy to implement. My ideas were basically a no-brainer, but before I discussed them with the entire market, I needed to test them on the best.

No surprises here. The meeting went as planned. The partners loved the ideas and felt they would enhance their profitability while at the same time be easy to implement. They would also actually cut through a lot of the red tape that had been tying their hands behind their backs. I asked them to test it out for the entire month and we would meet again to discuss their results in the next thirty days. I told them not to discuss this information with anyone until their results were in and we had sufficient data to support our suppositions. They all agreed.

The meeting had taken a little over two and half hours, but I was still on track to get back to the house, pick up Cindy, and get to Ja-Zon's by 11:00 a.m.

On the drive home, my thoughts did a reversal. Why did I want to leave?

I didn't have an answer to that. I felt peaceful, happy, and personally contented. I had spent the last two years honing this market. All the players were in place and producing results that to say the least, were impressive.

What did I have to gain in Boise, Idaho? What did I have left to prove to myself? I knew from my previous experience in Florida that opening a brand-new market is always a risk. What if I failed? What if something happened and I failed again? Did I really want to start over again? Maybe I was getting too old to continue playing this game of risk versus reward. I noticed I was white-knuckled and began to release my death grip on the steering wheel.

As I pulled into the driveway, I noted Cindy was outside waiting. Maybe she was a little anxious too. She got in my car and we headed over to Ja-Zon's.

Small talk consumed our somewhat nervous conversation. Cindy knew I was distracted, but she didn't pry. One of the many attributes that I truly appreciate about her is she never attempts to pry information out of me. Somehow she knows that when I am ready to share, I will.

I turned the corner and eased my BMW into a parking place right in front of Ja-Zon's business. Cindy looked at me in a curious way and said, "Are you ready?"

Turning, I looked at her and grinned. "You know me well enough to know I was born ready!"

We got out of the car and walked up to the front door. I opened the door for Cindy, took a deep breath, and followed her in.

Chapter 14
News Flash – My New Discovery

Ja-Zon greeted us warmly, as if the three of us were the only human beings on the planet. As we settled into the peaceful environment she had created, I began to relax. The conversation was lighthearted and reminded me of perhaps the type of conversation three old friends might have had in order to catch up on the past.

I saw a deck of tarot cards that had been conveniently placed on the coffee table As is my style, I asked Ja-Zon if she wanted me to shuffle the cards. She smiled at me and said, "Are you in a hurry?"

I couldn't help but smile back and say, "No, not really … well, maybe!"

She laughed aloud and said, "I love it. A world-class decision-maker who can't even make up his own mind." Now, Cindy was laughing too.

"Well, should I shuffle the cards or not?" I said impatiently.

They both began laughing so hysterically that I thought at any moment they might tumble off the couch they were sharing. I sat back and watched as the tears of laughter filled their eyes and flowed down their respective cheeks. Ja-Zon reached over to get a box of tissues, which she shared with Cindy.

As they began to dab their eyes, Ja-Zon said, "I am so sorry, Kevin. Please shuffle the cards at your leisure."

I replied, "Are you sure?" The laughing resumed.

Shaking my head from side to side, I picked up the deck and began to shuffle them. By the time I had finished, Cindy and Ja-Zon's composure had returned and the reading began.

Ja-Zon prayed to God and her guides for guidance. She prayed the information shared would be helpful and insightful. When she opened her eyes, she stated, "You and Cindy come searching for answers to a lot of questions you have pertaining to a crossroad you have recently come to. This crossroad combines personal direction and financial awareness. The guides are showing me a very strong desire in Kevin to want to move from Farmington." She then began to lay down the tarot cards in a fashion resembling a Celtic cross. She directed her first question at me. "Where do you want to move?"

I replied, "Boise, Idaho."

"Well, let's see what we will see," she passively stated. Her words were like an afterthought.

Suddenly she gasped, saying, "If you move to Boise, Idaho, it will mean financial ruin for you."

I quickly responded, "How can that be?"

All she said was "The market has changed. This is not the right time to make a move to Boise."

I was somewhat in a state of shock. My faith in what she was saying was certainly strong enough to believe what she was saying was true. Prying, I asked her, "What about moving up there in six to twelve months?"

"Nope, you have to make Farmington your home for the next two years!"

"Why is that?" I exclaimed.

"The guides are telling me you have to call Farmington your home for the next two years in order to meet a dark-haired woman."

I immediately resorted to my lower state of consciousness, wondering how Cindy might be feeling about that! "What does a dark-haired woman have to do with me?" I inquired.

She stated, "The guides are showing me a beautiful rainbow that will be connected after your meeting with her. It is imperative the two of you meet. The meeting will enhance your personal and business lives, spilling over and affecting many others in much the same way. Currently she is not here, but she will be moving here permanently within the next two years."

"Let me make sure I understand exactly what you are telling me. Moving to Boise, Idaho at this time will create a financial hardship on Cindy and me because the market has changed," I paraphrased.

"No, I said it would cause financial ruin for you because the market has changed!" she stated emphatically.

"Okay and the dark-haired women who I am to meet will not show up in Farmington for two years. So I must continue to live here until her arrival and then somehow, somewhere destiny will bring us together in order to complete some kind of metaphysical rainbow?"

"Kevin, the information I have given you has been sent to you from God via my guides. It is my job to interpret what they are telling me. The messages I have provided you are crystal-clear, specific, and precise. But as you already know, you have a free will and can choose what path you want to follow," she spouted in a loving way.

This is not what I had expected. I looked directly into Cindy's eyes and then I gazed into Ja-Zon's eyes. I really wanted the opportunity to take over the Boise market. I searched their eyes looking for a loophole or at least some glimmer of hope. Finding none, I sat back in the chair as my heart filled with despair and disappointment.

I suddenly became aware of the mystical music that had been playing in the background all this time. Just as suddenly, I also became aware Ja-Zon was speaking again, but I missed what she was saying because her voice seemed to be so far away. I interrupted her diplomatically, apologizing, and asked her politely if she would mind repeating what she had just said. Not missing a beat, she restated her comment. "As I said before, free will is at your command. Cindy and you may decide to walk out the front door, drive home, pack your stuff, and leave for Boise, Idaho tomorrow. All human beings on planet Earth have the ability to internally remap their own reality. It is your choice and always will be!" she responded.

I realized suddenly I had my loophole. It was my choice. It had to be my choice; no other way would work. I was the one in charge of my life.

I returned quickly to my cheerful self. Smiling, I stood up, gave Ja-Zon a big ol' bear hug, walked to the front door, and then waited as Ja-Zon whispered something to Cindy. They finished hugging and we bid her goodbye.

On the way home, Cindy asked me what my impression was of the reading.

Not wanting to give her more information than I thought she needed, I told her I was very impressed, adding it was a lot to digest. She agreed but quickly stated her feelings regarding Boise. Obviously I just listened. My unstated agenda was just a little different.

I slept well that night, dreaming of Boise, Idaho. I awoke very early and prepared to make the three-hour drive to Albuquerque. Bobby was always early, so I wanted to be sure not to be late.

I was standing out on the top deck enjoying the early morning sunrise when Cindy joined me. "You were up bright and very early this morning." she commented.

Offhandedly I said, "Yeah, I wanted to be sure to catch this sunrise before I left."

She ignored my comment and proceeded. "Listen, I just wanted you to know that whatever you decide to do is fine with me." I turned away from the sunrise to look at her. Cindy's long blond hair was beginning to shimmer as the sun's rays were just breaking the horizon. She took my breath away as I envisioned her pure innocence.

"Thanks, but this decision has *we* written all over it not just *me*," I replied.

"Really," she said. "I had the feeling after the reading yesterday you had already made your decision to go to Boise. I was just letting you know I would support you." Her eyes began filling with tears. I took her in my arms and tried to explain how important her input was. She held me tightly and whispered six words in my ear: "The market has changed … financial ruin."

I got to the Marriot hotel around ten thirty in the morning. Very pleased with myself, I got out of the car, lit a cigarette, grabbed my folder, and headed for the bar.

Sure enough, as I entered the bar, there was Bobby motioning me over. It seemed to me he was studying me as I walked over to him. As expected at that time of the morning, we had the place to ourselves. "Good morning, Bob. How was the drive up from Las Cruces?" I asked.

"I had some business to take care of here yesterday, so I drove up Monday morning and then spent the night," he replied. "How are you?"

"If I was any better, I'd be twins!" I stated.

He laughed as I reached into my folder, pulling out the information I had compiled. "I see you have been busy," he quipped.

I told him I had been in touch with the chamber of commerce in Boise and that they had overnighted some great information to me. That is when he stopped me dead in my tracks. "Listen, Kev, I have been doing my own research and I have decided not to go into the Boise market!" he summarized.

I was just a little flabbergasted. I thought I might know the answer, but I had to hear it from Bobby's own lips. Softly, almost coyly, I asked, "Why not?"

Without a moment's hesitation, *he* responded, *"The market has changed!"*

Sitting there dumbfounded, my mind kind of went numb. He went on to explain how another franchisee and he had been looking into the market. He continued explaining that the other franchisee had signed an agreement with SONIC Industries since we had last spoken, procuring and protecting the best locations in the city of Boise. He stated that trying to go into Boise now would be *too big of a financial risk!* It was a risk that he was not willing to take and a risk certainly too big for him to allow me to take.

By now, you, the reader, know me well enough to probably know what my next question was going to be, huh. "So, Bobby, what you are saying is if we went into Boise in the near future, it could mean *financial ruin* for me?"

"That is what I am saying, absolutely! Your pockets are not deep enough to handle even one store that fails, much less two or three in a row, which is a very real possibility the way the market is currently!"

When I got home that night, Cindy was very anxious to know what had happened. I told her the entire story. She remained silent, listening to every word as I recounted my conversation with Bobby. When I had finished, she asked me how I felt. I explained to her I no longer had the desire to go to Boise. Duh! I also told her that although Ja-Zon had stated I had free will, sometimes beyond our comprehension, God intervenes for our own good.

Then it dawned on me. It wasn't God intervening; it was my God self at work again. He had been very busy rearranging my life again. He definitely had a purpose. Secretly I wondered what he had in store for me. Bobby had confirmed what Ja-Zon and her guides had predicted. These words kept popping up in my head: "oh, ye have so little faith." I thought I understood.

Chapter 15
Curiosity, Faith, Belief, Knowing

I wondered why four words—*curiosity, faith, belief,* and *knowing*—kept cropping up in my thoughts. I decided to do some Bible research.

As I read over the four gospels—Matthew, Mark, Luke, and John—I realized I wasn't the only human being on the planet whose faith from time to time was not what it could be. In all four gospels it had been recorded that Jesus rebuked his twelve disciples over and over again for their lack of faith.

In the gospel of John, chapter fourteen, Christ speaks to his disciples, trying to explain to them, in loving way, to not let their hearts be troubled because he would be leaving soon and they would not be able to follow him.

This confused Thomas and Phillip. Thomas told Jesus they didn't understand where he was going, so how would they know the way? Christ answered him, in verse six and seven, saying, "I, am the way, the truth, and the life: No MAN cometh unto the Father, but by me. If ye had known me, ye should have known my Father also: and from henceforth, ye know him, and have seen him."

Phillip still didn't get it and asked Jesus to show them the Father, which would help suffice them. In verse nine I could tell Jesus was getting a little impatient with his disciples when he said, "Have I been so long time with you, and yet hast thou not known me, Phillip? He that hath seen me hath seen the Father; and how sayest thou then, show us the Father?"

Christ continues in verses ten, eleven, twelve, and thirteen:

"Believest thou not that I am in the Father, and the Father in me? The words that I speak unto you I speak not of myself: but the Father that dwelleth in me, he doeth the works."

"Believe me that I am in the Father, and the Father in me: or else believe me for the very works' sake."

"Verily, verily, I say unto you, He that believeth on me, the works that I do shall he do also; and greater works than these shall he do; because I go unto my Father."

"And whatsoever ye shall ask in my name, that will I do, that the Father may be glorified in the Son."

With a fresh set of eyes and a lot more faith, I began to fully understand what Jesus was trying to get across to his disciples. Jesus the man was powerless and he knew it. His unquestionable power came from connecting his physical self with his God self while remaining conscious throughout the process. He learned to do this so often that by the time he started preaching, Jesus the son of man could not be separated, except on rare occasions, from Christ, the son of God.

What I thought was even more exciting was the message Christ tried to deliver to his disciples: if their faith was strong enough, they too could perform miracles and even greater works than he did. In verse seventeen, Christ once again confirmed the world's humanness and the disciples' spirituality when he stated:

"Even the Spirit of truth; whom the world cannot receive, because it SEETH him not, neither KNOWETH him: But ye know him, for he dwelleth with you, and shall be in you."

So I pondered, if I am a human being living in a lower state of consciousness, then I would naturally believe that if I can't see it, smell it, touch it, taste it, or hear it, I might not be aware that *it* exists. Becoming aware I was a spiritual being having a human experience, this started to make sense to me.

Most gentile and Judeo-Christians believe as I do—that Christ was able to suspend and defy the laws of nature at his will. Too many firsthand accounts of the miracles Christ performed were witnessed and recorded to deny his ability to suspend and defy the laws of nature as we know them to be. These eyewitness accounts are the base from which we launched our curiosity in manifesting the faith, believing Christ was the son of God incarnate.

As I reflected upon the four gospels, I noted Jesus always gave credit to whom it was due, God the Father. Jesus the man was ego-free, knowing in his human consciousness that he was almost totally connected to his God self, created in the likeness and image of God the Father.

One of the few times an observer, past or present, might be able to bisect Jesus humanness from his spiritual Christ self was in the Garden of Gethsemane when he prayed to God, "to let this cup pass before him," knowing if God didn't pardon him, he would be terribly tortured, humiliated, and finally crucified unmercifully the following day.

Jesus prayed the same prayer three times that night, pleading that although as a human being he did not want to go through this, ultimately he knew God's will must be done.

As was foretold, Christ was crucified and then resurrected himself on the third day, physically revealing himself to his disciples and others on numerous occasions and in several locations.

No other human being in recorded history has died a physical death and then been seen in the flesh after resurrecting himself. The resurrection of Jesus Christ is the foundation of Christianity. To deny him as a deity would be to deny knowing my spirit and its connection to God.

I decided to embrace my new perspective in an attempt to live my life in a more Christ like manner. Some areas of my life improved greatly, while other areas continued to struggle miserably. Most observers would never be able to see the difference in either arena. I knew I was on to something special; I just didn't know how to pull it all together yet.

The Spring, Summer, and Fall of 2001

Spring and summer are a very busy time for people in the restaurant industry, especially people who work at SONIC drive-ins. The partners are always busy hiring and training new employees in early spring to be to ready for the sales influx that coincides with the temperature reaching into the high sixties. Additionally, we normally paint the outside of the buildings, stripe the parking lots, and begin planting a variety of flowers in and around each of the properties. The curbside appeal is extremely important to the continued success of all our restaurants. We worked hard to maintain this image.

Late spring and early summer was extraordinary because it afforded to me the opportunity to meet and greet the new kids who had been hired. I really enjoyed observing those smiling new faces with their excited eyes, because I realized that from this pool of talent my management teams would be able to grow and I would then harvest many of our future leaders.

Sometimes we were fortunate enough to hire back some very productive folks who, for one reason or another, had decided to seek employment elsewhere. I always viewed this as our opportunity to prove to these folks how valuable they had been to the success of our overall organization.

Another positive aspect of rehiring people was the skill levels those folks obtained while working for us previously. Additionally, perhaps those previously employed were more mature now and ready for some new challenges! I not only supported this stance but looked upon rehiring as a reunion. It always excited and inspired me when I had the chance to see some old faces reappear.

In the spring of 2001, Bobby requested that my regional director, Martin Romero, take over the Colorado market. This meant Martin would have too many restaurants and he would have to give up some of his restaurant responsibilities. Since he was living in Santa Fe, New Mexico and overseeing forty plus restaurants in and around Santa Fe, Albuquerque, and Farmington, I suspected the Farmington market—which stretched as far south as Gallup to as far north as Durango, Colorado—would be the logical choice. I don't know who made the final decision, but Farmington turned out to be the market Martin had to give up.

Since October of 1995, Martin had been my regional director. Over the years we had developed a very good personal and business relationship. I liked his leadership style and respected his perspective. His directives made good sense and were always crystal clear. He was very successful and secure in his position. I liked that. As in most successful relationships, we respected and trusted each other in all matters. I found it easy to give him my complete loyalty. Although I would miss him, I knew the Colorado market was struggling and needed his help.

In the past year, Martin had made sporadic trips to Colorado in an attempt to give the supervisors and management teams some support. The two main leaders in Denver and Colorado Springs had made the decision to become SONIC franchisees, which put a tremendous strain on the management teams and a couple of young, inexperienced supervisors. I knew most of the folks in Colorado, and felt they just needed some guidance and inspiration. Hopefully Martin would get it done.

I was a little bit nervous about who Bobby would choose to replace Martin.

When I found out it was Norvell Barnes, I was somewhat relieved. Norv and his wife, Terri, lived in stunning Silver City, New Mexico. They were highly successful SONIC Drive-In owner-operators. Norv was also one of Bobby's old guard and Terri was Bobby's sister-in-law.

The old guards were guys like Ted Sprinkle and Martin Romero, who had put in a lot of time and hard work at becoming very successful. In doing so, they became elite members of Bobby's inner circle.

You might think, being married to the sister of Betty Merritt (Bobby's wife), Norv would receive a free pass into the inner circle. It didn't work that way.

A matter of fact, Bobby expected more from family members on a daily basis than he did from anyone else. It did not take me long to figure out people must earn their positions within the old guard by protecting the king and his assets. Bobby is a very giving person by nature; however, he does not lavish his trust on everyone, only the old guard.

I thought I was in a pretty good position since the only old guard I had ever had a real serious conflict with was J.D. Merritt, Bobby's brother. And that had been four and half years ago. Besides that, Martin had been fairly tied up for the past year in the Colorado market and I was used to having very little supervision.

Then along came Norvell, a newly promoted regional director with all kinds of vim and vigor. Sometimes folks who are given more authority do not respond with the correct amount of force necessary to accomplish what they would like to; case in point, Norvell Barnes. It took about six weeks for Norv and me to get on the same sheet of music. Ted and Norvell never did.

Needless to say, there was a lot of unnecessary pain and suffering. Ted and I had developed a very specific way of overseeing the market, and Norvell didn't agree with our techniques or tactics. He did not believe one supervisor could oversee eleven restaurants effectively and be ready to open number twelve within a few months. All the information I gave him reflected his miscalculations, but he didn't want to change his stance.

Ultimately his goal was to split the market, giving Ted responsibility for the five outlying stores south of Farmington, and I would pick up the remaining seven. I knew this was not a good move and tried my best to prevent it.

In late summer we had a supervisors' meeting just north of Albuquerque. Eddie Saroch, a regional vice president (RVP) with SONIC Industries, presented a new technique for determining how much profit the entire SONIC system was leaving on the table. On the surface his presentation made sense, but it also had many flaws.

I was not surprised when most of the Merritt group bought into it, because he is a great presenter—dramatically convincing. After the meeting I questioned Eddie at great length regarding some of the flaws I saw in his presentation. He admitted that saving the sum of money he talked about would entail running nearly flawless operations, which he stated was not a reasonable consideration. He said, "There are too many intangibles, especially pertaining to labor" to meet the assumptions he had presented.

I asked him why he did not take the intangibles into consideration during his presentation, and he said, "The goal was to awaken everyone to the possibilities that were available." I told him I knew the Merritt group well enough to know they would attempt to surpass his expectations, which could ultimately hurt sales and possibly the brand itself. He disagreed, stating the Merritt franchise was a smart company that would recognize where the opportunity was to pick up extra profit dollars without jeopardizing store sales or the brand. I knew I was not going to win this discussion.

Sure enough, two months later Ted and I were sitting in a restaurant with Norvell and Nick Stamnos (Bobby's son-in-law, and the director of operations over the entire Merritt group), going over my profit and loss statements for 2001. For two and half hours they drilled me in an attempt to convince me I had left a large amount of profit on the table over the past ten months. Fortunately, as the conversation began to get heated up, Nick received a phone call he had to take, so Ted, Norvell, and myself took a much-needed break. Norv walked away from the table to make a phone call.

Ted saw someone he knew in the bar area and walked over to talk to him, and I went looking for the bathroom. As I stood there taking care of business, I started thinking about the previous two and half hours I had wasted while I had listened to Nick and Norvell rant and rave. The only tools they purposed using to squeeze more profit out of the stores were the hammer and chisel Eddie Saroch had provided them at the supervisors' retreat. They were on a mission, and frankly I knew nothing I had to say was going to sway them.

Our budgets did not reflect this new thinking. We had spent a lot of time developing them in January, and now, ten months into the calendar year, upper management had developed a new plan. This plan was a knee-jerk reaction to Eddie Saroch's pie-in-the-sky supposition. Prior to this, the financial goal had always been to be better in sales and profit than we had been the year before. For the past three straight years, the Farmington market had seen double-digit increases in both sales and profits. At the end of this calendar year, I was projecting a sales increase of 1,483,000 dollars. That would be a whopping 14 percent increase in revenue.

The same eleven stores' estimated profit would be up over 27 percent or 319,964 dollars in additional profit, compared to the previous year of 2000.

As stood over the sink washing my hands, I caught myself looking into the eyes of a very angry man. My ego had been tweaked. I was frustrated, confused, and stressed to the max. I didn't like me very much when I was in this state of mind, but I didn't know how to control the man in the mirror.

By the time I had finished washing up; my nerves were stretched like a rubber band.

I knew Nick and Norvell were just following Bobby and Eddie's directives, but I also felt what had been accomplished the last four years didn't seem to matter. I went back to the table and sat there waiting patiently. Nick was the first one to return to the table. I looked him straight in the eyes and calmly told him I was quitting. He looked surprised and asked me why. I told him I could no longer work for a company that did not appreciate what I did for it.

I explained to him I was more than willing to stay through the end of the year or until he found my replacement. The fireworks began instantaneously!

Nick lashed out in Stamnos fashion, asking what he was to do while I was out looking for another job. I told him that if he didn't think I was professional enough to do my job to the best of my ability, he should fire me right there!

Ted and Norv strolled up to the table just as I was finishing my comment.

As they were sitting down, Nick stood up. He grabbed his cell phone while looking directly at Ted and asked, "Did you know about this?"

Ted replied, "Know about what?"

Nick spun around and started to walk away. Over his shoulder he muttered, "He just quit!"

For just a few seconds, you could have heard a cotton ball hit the floor. The color in Ted's cheeks was gone. Norvell looked like he had just been struck by a New Mexico lightening bolt. It took few seconds before the initial shock wore off.

During the fifteen minutes or so Nick was gone, Ted and Norvell tried to interrogate me, but I had pretty much shut down. I was numb all over. I knew Nick was talking to Bobby. I couldn't believe I had allowed myself to get so mad that I had quit. I knew at this point Nick would rather see me gone than try to work things out. A smart person doesn't talk to Nick Stamnos the way I had and survive, unless Bobby gets involved. I figured the longer Nick was gone, the better my chances were going to be. If Bobby would provide just enough wiggle room for me, I might be able to recant.

Amazingly enough, Nick returned to the table with a new kind of attitude.

He was friendly and upbeat when he asked Ted and Norvell to politely leave the table. He and I then went back over the profit and loss statements but this time from a perspective that was less threatening and intimidating. This was the Nick Stamnos I respected and enjoyed being around. He showed genuine concern and appeared to be more willing to see my perspective

Even though my position was closely guarded, it was obvious Bobby had provided plenty of wiggle room. Nick never acknowledged or brought up the issue of my quitting. It was like I had never mentioned it. When we parted ways that evening, I was fortunately still employed.

Neither Ted nor Norvell ever brought this situation up again in my presence. Perhaps they were just relieved Bobby was able to convince Nick that the hard-to-manage Kevin McPeek, Sr. was still of some value to the organization. It didn't take much time to determine how much value Bobby Merritt would put on my plate.

CHAPTER 16
Ya gotta be ready when you go to Gallup

Ted finished directing the completion of the new store in Gallup around mid-November, 2001. Even though September 11 was still fresh on everybody's mind, Ted was bound and determined to finish his project on time.

We had been open about two weeks when Bobby showed up unexpectedly.

In all the years I had known Bobby, he had never missed coming to personally see how things were going whenever we opened a new drive-in. He invited me to dinner that night. Operationally the store was running very smoothly, so I accepted his invitation.

He took me to one of his favorite restaurants in Gallup. About halfway through the meal, our conversation shifted from being fun and casual to one that got serious and right to the point.

He explained that under the current conditions Martin Romero was having a difficult time getting the Colorado market under control. Privately I thought what they had been asking Martin to accomplish was almost impossible with all of his responsibilities, Martin could only spend just a few days out of the month in Colorado, and that wasn't fair to Martin or the market.

No sooner had this thought crossed my mind when Bobby stated he felt they had put Martin in an impossible position. He had discussed this with Martin and Martin had agreed. Bobby mentioned they had offered the Colorado market to Martin but he had turned it down.

Bobby told me there were several supervisors who were interested in the position. He said that if I was interested, I would have to go through a formal interviewing process that would take place in Las Cruces. If I wanted, he could set it up for the coming week. He also said Cindy was more than welcome to come along for the two-to-three day process. He stated the decision would be made very quickly because whoever was selected would have to be prepared to move to Colorado the first part of January.

I sat there fascinated and speechless. Less than two weeks ago I had had a blowup with Nick Stamnos, and now I was being given the opportunity to apply and interview for the position of a regional director. I wondered silently if this was just some varnish Bobby wanted to spread around to cover up the surface cracks that had been exposed a couple of weeks ago.

Bobby interrupted my thought process when he interjected that an important part of the application process would be submitting a detailed brief stating and then summarizing why I would make a good regional director.

I decided to test the seriousness of Bobby's intention when I told him I didn't think I could sell my house in thirty days. He stated that if I was selected his company would purchase my house for the appraised value. This offer was no doubt a serious one. I asked him how long I had to write the brief and then proceed with the interviewing process. He said the brief needed to be faxed to the home office by Monday and the interviewing process would begin on Thursday. The decision would be made no later than Friday.

I felt like I had been caught up in a Texas whirlwind. On one hand, this was an opportunity I had dreamed of, but on the other hand,

I didn't think it was very fair to have so little time to prepare a response. I decided to calculate my reply with a carefully measured delaying tactic.

I told Bobby that before I would be willing to commit to going through the application and interviewing process, I would have to discuss the possible outcome of this action with Cindy. She would have to be not only willing but enthusiastic about moving to Colorado prior to me making a commitment to go through the application and interviewing process he had already outlined. He agreed but pushed his timeline. I stated that if Cindy was excited about the possibility of moving to Colorado, I could have the brief done by Monday and we would be in Las Cruces the following Wednesday.

On our way back to the drive-in, Bobby said if I was selected I could relinquish my job responsibilities around the fifteenth of December. If I needed more time to make my arrangements, I could delay getting up to Colorado till the first or second week in January. I was pleased to know there was some flexibility within his timeline. I told him at this point I didn't know how much time would be needed; however, I appreciated his flexibility.

We got back to the SONIC Drive-In around ten thirty that night. Bobby took the time to talk to every manager and each employee individually. I watched as he acknowledged and appreciated their hard work. Here was a man with a wonderful gift: the natural ability to make people around him feel good about themselves and the work they perform. Once again, I was proud to be in the presence of this truly great man.

After he had finished talking with everyone, I walked with him outside. As he started to get into his car, he looked me directly in the eye, stating, "I hope you make the right decision. The folks in Colorado deserve your talent and keen insights. I look forward to reading your brief." He smiled broadly, got into his car, and headed toward Las Cruces.

It appeared obvious to me that if I wanted the position, all I needed to do was apply for it. It was my impression that if we were willing to move to Colorado and take some risk, the job would be mine. I was certain he wanted me to know this before he left Gallup. I lit up a cigarette, inhaling deeply while I contemplated my options. I knew Ted was kicking around the idea of retiring someday, but neither a timeline nor a deadline had ever been proposed or discussed. I knew that when he did I would be in a position of potential wealth.

The opportunity in Colorado would be somewhat risky, though not as risky as opening a new market, because nineteen drive-ins were already open with plenty of history to work from. The twentieth drive-in was scheduled to open in north Denver sometime in mid-February. The challenge would be boosting profits. The eleven-store market in Farmington was projected to do 600,000 dollars more in profit than the combined nineteen stores in Colorado, but it had not always been that way. Up until two and half years ago, the Colorado market had been the leading market within the Merritt group. In my gut I knew what was holding this market back. If my gut was right, this market could be turned around before the end of the first quarter of 2002.

It was twelve thirty that night before I had unfrozen all the possibilities and balanced all the logical consequences. Although it was late, I decided to call Cindy. I had a two-hour drive a head of me before I got home, and I was certain she would be fast asleep before then. I took a chance she might still be awake and dialed the number.

I was relieved when she answered the phone right after the first ring. She sounded sleepy when she said, "Hello."

"You sound like I just woke you up," I responded.

She laughed. "Not really. I've been dozing on and off for the past hour. What's up? Have you left Gallup yet?"

Two questions in two sentences! She was awake now! "I'm just wrapping things up here, and then I am heading home," I stated.

"It's so late. Why don't you just spend the night in Gallup and drive home tomorrow morning?" she asked. "Besides, you know how much I worry about you driving home so late at night, don't you?"

"I know, I know you worry, but I don't have the time to spend the night in Gallup," I reported. "Besides, I'm not tired. As a matter of fact, I'm all jacked up! Bobby showed up tonight and took me out to dinner. He asked me if I would be interested in applying and interviewing for a regional director position that is opening up in Colorado the first of next year!" I blurted out.

I could hear the excitement in her voice when she said, "You've got to be kidding. How wonderful would that be?"

So I asked, "You would be willing to move again?"

I could hear the smile in her voice when she stated that although it had been almost four years since we had moved to Farmington, she was more than willing to support a move to Colorado!

I gave her a brief but very precise overview of the coming week's agenda. I could feel her excitement. Just as I told her I would be home around 3:00 a.m., my cell phone died. I walked briskly to my car, and just as I plugged the phone into the charger, it rang. It was Cindy reminding me to be careful coming home. I thanked her and told her to sleep well.

I then followed that phone call up with one to Ted. Both he and Sherry were night owls, so I didn't feel like I would be intruding on them. Ted answered and we had an excellent discussion pertaining the information Bobby had provided me. Ted gave me some valuable insights regarding this opportunity. And although I got the feeling he would have preferred that I stay, I knew he would support and guide me through this process, if indeed I was offered the position and then decided to take the promotion.

Overall I felt very good about his responses and reaction.

I left Gallup, New Mexico early that Sunday morning wondering if it would be for the last time. As I headed north on Highway 666, I saw two shooting stars cross the horizon just in front of me. I wondered if this was a sign of things to come.

Chapter 17
The Dark-Haired Woman Arrives

I pulled into the garage around 3:00 a.m. and decided to go straight to my office to write the first draft of my brief. I opened the french doors to enter the office and flipped on the ceiling light. Instead of sitting down at my desk, I walked over to the sliding glass door. I slid it open just enough for me to walk out onto the semi-private, second-story covered deck.

I was feeling a little discombobulated and thought the chill of the early morning would be a good antidote. I sat down on one of the overstuffed red wood rockers, planting my feet firmly upon an ottoman. The next thing I remember was the smell of a freshly lit cigarette and the aroma of Cindy's specially brewed coffee.

I ever so slowly opened one eye, and I realized that sometime during the early morning hours Cindy had covered me with a thick quilt. As my eyes adjusted to the morning rays, I saw her standing by the railing, sipping her coffee and gazing out into the distance.

"Good morning, honey," I quietly stated. "Thanks for the quilt. It was pretty chilly last night."

As she turned to look at me all warm and toasty, she said, "You're more than welcome. I heard you come in last night, and when you didn't come to bed, I figured you had gone straight to your office. I came down to check on you and found you fast asleep. You looked so peaceful I didn't want to wake you up, so I covered you with the quilt. I knew you had to be exhausted!"

I lit up a cigarette and asked her what time it was. She said it was about seven thirty. I told her my intent had been to get started writing my first draft of the brief Bobby was requiring. She smiled broadly.

"Have you been up all night?" I asked.

"Pretty much," she responded. "After I tucked you in, I decided to just stay up."

"Gee, I'm really sorry. I never dreamed there was any way you'd still be awake. I should have made sure of it, though. It was pretty thoughtless of me," I stated apologetically.

"Hey, no big deal. I was just glad to know you were home safely."

We continued talking on the deck until around nine that morning. On the way upstairs, we realized we were hungry. I suggested doing brunch at one of the local hotels. Cindy agreed, suggesting we invite Ted and Sherry. I thought that was an excellent idea and set it up for noon.

Sherry's Serendipity

After I had showered and shaved, I felt like a new man. Rejuvenated, I went down to my office, made a few necessary phone calls, and wrote the first draft of my brief. As I reread what I had written, I felt pretty good about it. I knew it needed some polishing, but overall it stated basically what needed to be said. Besides, it was Saturday and I had till Monday afternoon to complete it.

I looked at my watch and hurriedly went back upstairs to find Cindy. I had lost track of the time. Fortunately, she was ready. We gathered what we needed and left for the hotel.

We arrived just before Ted and Sherry pulled in. We waited for them at the front door of the hotel. As they approached I noted that Ted looked a little tired, but Sherry appeared to be her normal bubbling self. I wondered if Ted had told Sherry about the possibility of Cindy and me moving to Colorado. We exchanged hugs and entered the hotel.

As anticipated, the brunch was superb. After making several trips through the five different serving lines, the four of us were well fed and satisfied.

Smiling from ear to ear, Sherry was the first to pull out her cigarettes.

Before the filter touched her lips, Ted's lighter was in his hand, waiting. She turned, leaning in slightly, allowing him access. I had seen this routine many times. They had perfected their technique. Ted then lit up, inhaling deeply.

We wasted no time in following their lead. I know this is not a politically correct statement, but nothing in this world tastes or smells as good as a freshly lit cigarette right after a fantastic meal. It is too bad smokers cannot limit themselves to just one cigarette after meals. It would eliminate many of our social and healthcare problems.

Our conversation was quite lively, bouncing around from one subject to another. At one point we were all laughing so hard I began having terrible stomach pains. Laughter is supposed to be wonderful for one's digestive system, so I dismissed the pain. As expected, the pain went away as quickly as it had surfaced.

Somewhere along the way, we arrived at our destination, Colorado. The mood turned sober and everyone seemed to be picking their words carefully.

We all knew this was an important decision—possibly a life-changing decision—and no one at the table was taking it lightly. Cindy and I would later agree Ted and Sherry were being very supportive. Their words of encouragement and empowerment were appreciated.

Sherry did suggest that before we made a final decision it would be smart to contact Mary Ross for a reading. Mary had recently moved to Farmington and was living with them. Sherry explained that Mary had been in India for almost two years, studying with Sai BaBa, a very well-known Indian swami.

According to Sherry, Mary's readings were very accurate and extremely powerful. I offhandedly thanked her, explaining that I would make sure to put it on the list of things I needed to get done. Sherry let it go at that.

When we parted ways in the parking lot, my perception was the four of us were all on the same dance floor. That may have been true, but I was the only fool not dancing. I mention this only because I was so consumed about reining in the opportunity to become the regional director in Colorado I had consciously forgotten the last spiritual reading Cindy and I had received from Ja-Zon, which stated *I was not to leave Farmington before I met with a dark-haired woman*. Even though I had forgotten, it did not stop the dark-haired woman from arriving in Farmington, just as foretold to me, two years prior. Throughout the month of December, 2002, I would be encouraged by many to meet with Mary Ross.

Chapter 18
La Cruces, New Mexico

I finished writing my brief and faxed it to Bobby's personal fax machine. I felt good because it had been completed two days earlier than the deadline date. This would give me Sunday, Monday, and Tuesday to take care any market concerns before Cindy and I left for Las Cruces Wednesday morning.

As it turned out, nothing unexpected arose. We packed Tuesday night and left for the land of crosses early Wednesday morning. We arrived in Las Cruces late that afternoon and went straight to the office.

It wasn't often I had the opportunity to actually get to see the wonderful folks whose dedication to the job enabled them to provide such great support to those of us who were in operations. I had never seen so few do so much for so many. It was always a pleasure for me to deal with these highly skilled and marvelously trained decision-makers.

After Cindy and I made our rounds, we were able to meet with Barbie Stammer (president of the Merritt Group). She gave me an overview of the next day's agenda as well as directions to the hotel where our room reservations were. After some small talk, she offered to take us to her favorite Mexican restaurant for dinner. One would have to be a fool not to accept that invitation. Nobody on the planet knows Mexican food like Barbie does. Naturally we accepted, and as expected, we were not disappointed.

The following day was slated for interviewing. I met with Barbie and Nick in the morning. I was surprised when we sat down together and Barbie stated that she and Nick had read over my brief, which had answered all their questions, and they were wondering if I had any questions for them. I was caught off guard and had expected to be drilled on numerous fronts. Instead the interview wound up being an informal chat. After I left Barbie's office, I knew the regional director position was mine. Nothing was stated outright, but the interview was way too casual to mean anything else but that. Then I got to thinking that perhaps it was casual because they had already decided on someone else. Perhaps they were just being nice, allowing me to go through the process in order for me to feel appreciated. After all, I had only been with the company six and half years. Maybe I hadn't paid enough dues to actually be considered for such an important position. As badly as I wanted the position, I knew I would be okay with either decision.

I felt very peaceful as wandered around the office looking for Cindy. I found her talking to Leslie Berryman. "Hey, you girls want to go to lunch," I asked.

Leslie responded, "So, how did it go?"

"To tell you the truth, Leslie, I really don't know," I stated,

She coyly smiled and winked at me. "Oh, I think you know. You just don't want to say, do you?"

"Honestly, I don't have a clue," I said softly.

She turned to face Cindy, each of them smiling at each other, and said, "We would be foolhardy not to promote Kev, 'cause everything he touches turns to gold."

"Thanks, Leslie, for your vote of confidence. It's too bad you are not on the voting committee," I whispered.

"What makes you think that I am not on the voting committee?" she whispered back.

"Because, I didn't have to interview with you," I calmly stated.

"Well, you forget I am the CFO of this company, and I do have a vote, especially on an important decision like this one. You didn't have to interview with me or any of the other officers because we already know what a wonderful asset you would be for the Colorado market! And besides, we didn't want to waste your time," she hastily replied. "Now why don't you get out of here and take your lovely wife out to lunch. I would love to join you, but I promised Bob I would have this proposal to him as soon as possible." Still smiling, she added, "I'm certain I will get to see you before you leave town."

As Cindy and I were leaving the office, she cocked her head a little to the side and said in a very peppy way, "Looks like we should make plans to move to Colorado, huh?" I nudged her a bit as we walked toward the car. "Ya think so," I said with a little sarcasm in my voice. She just smiled knowingly.

After lunch we returned to the office and literally bumped into Stella Rodriguez as she rounded the corner of the entrance to the lobby. Stella is another secret weapon in the Merritt arsenal. She not only takes enormous pride in her work, but she is also a timeline perfectionist. If you need something done correctly, in a timely manner, she's your gal.

As I was saying, Stella came bounding around the corner and came to a screeching halt before the three of us collided. Smiling broadly, she stated with laughter in her voice, "Oops, the big guy told me to find you guys, not run you guys over. Its so nice to see the both of you." We returned her warm greeting with some small talk as she guided us to Bobby's office. Just before we entered his office, she whispered to me in a very hushed voice, "Congratulations!"

I smiled at her and whispered back, "For what?" She returned my smile and gave me a hug, stating, "You'll make a great regional director for the Merritt group," and then she spun around and was gone. I wondered if Bobby had made the announcement while Cindy and I were at lunch. I turned around and Cindy was gone too! I found her in Bobby's office; she and Bobby were chit-chatting away as I walked in.

He waited for me to sit down and get comfortable. Then in the privacy of his office he made it official. No hoopla or fancy phrasing; just "Congratulations, I am sure you will do a great job in Colorado." I thanked him, stating I was looking forward to the challenge.

The following two days Bobby and I spent negotiating my deal. Cindy and I left for home on Saturday morning. We stopped in Albuquerque to see some of our dear friends, wound up spending the night, and returned to Farmington late Sunday morning.

As I began unpacking from the trip, I sat down on the bed, taking a moment to reflect on the past week. Everything I had envisioned had happened. I felt at peace with my life. I knew I had made the correct decision. There was absolutely no doubt in my mind, I would have the opportunity to help many regain their posture and refuel their desires. All I had to do was convey my ideas by teaching, coaching, and mentoring unselfishly.

I FINALLY MEET THE DARK-HAIRED WOMAN

With a little less than a month before the move, we had plenty to do. The first topic on my agenda was professional in nature. I wanted to ensure Ted and I completed a smooth transition. He had done a lot for me, and I wanted to make certain he was set up for success before I left. So I gathered up all the information pertaining to my stores and set up a meeting with him.

We met at his office and discussed at length our people and equipment resources. We revisited the budgets for the first quarter of 2002. He and I both felt very comfortable with the strategy that was in place. We decided the best timing for my last official day should be the fifteenth of December, the night of the manager's Christmas party. Saying goodbye to everyone at such a festive event appealed to me.

While I was busy taking care of SONIC business, Cindy was preoccupied with packing and contacting real estate agents and lenders in Colorado Springs. At night we would sit down and review the information she was gathering. It became apparent buying a house in Colorado was not only going to be a lot more expensive than we anticipated; finding the right one was going to be much more time-consuming as well.

We finally decided the smart thing to do was to not let this move stress us both out. Owning a home in Colorado was important to both of us; however, as an alternative, we could rent a place to stay until Cindy found exactly what she wanted. We would just pack up all our stuff and put it in storage until we found the home we wanted. No big deal. We could drive up to Colorado Springs and look around with the intent of buying without feeling the pressure to do so. I had another idea too. I knew she was putting a great deal of pressure on herself to get everything packed up before Christmas. I asked her if she felt this was a good time of the year to be trying to get this done.

She agreed with me it was not. I suggested we spend the next ten to twelve days shopping for Christmas and forget about packing until after the first of the year. She liked the idea on one hand, but the on the other hand, she stated she wouldn't be ready to make the move on time. I reminded her that Bobby was buying our house, so therefore we wouldn't have a deadline to be out of the house. She could take her time packing without feeling the pressure of a timeline. Cindy thought about it for a few minutes and then smiled in agreement. Then with a hint of sarcasm and a gleam in her eye, she stated, "You have such a brilliant mind! You knew you would figure out a way to keep from having to help me pack, didn't you?"

I acted surprised, laughing out loud, stating, "You know I never focus on how things get done; I only concentrate on who does them! You just happen to be the one who does them this time."

Smiling, she asked if I had any other fine ideas. I asked her if she wanted to spend Christmas in Denver.

"Do you really think we can?"

"Yeah, absolutely," I responded. "I can finish up everything I need to get done prior to the Christmas party. Since you don't have to worry about getting everything packed up before Christmas, I think we can fit a little vacation time in while we are in Colorado." Her smile broadened. "That sounds wonderful. I am so excited about getting to spend Christmas in Colorado!"

As planned, we left for Colorado Springs the day after the Christmas party.

Since it was mid-December and we would be driving four hundred miles through the Rocky Mountains, I obtained the weather forecast for southern Colorado. Fortune smiled upon us. Clear roads and beautiful sunny blue skies awaited our departure. Even though the forecast was favorable, I decided to leave two hours before sunrise. My reasoning behind this was based upon my experience and knowledge of the strange weather patterns that can change in an instant when driving on mountainous terrain. My other concern was that this time of the year the sun began to set around three o'clock in the afternoon. Even though the most treacherous part of the trip was only three hours away, Wolf Creek Pass could never be underestimated. If for some reason we didn't make it through the pass, we would have to turn around and head south to Santa Fe, New Mexico in order to catch Interstate 25 north. The stretch of road between Pagosa Springs and Santa Fe could be dangerous too. If we couldn't get through the pass, it was going to be an extremely long day.

We drove north on Highway 550 to Durango and then headed west on Highway 160, arriving at just about sunrise in Pagosa Springs. We found a little quaint restaurant just on the outskirts of town and ate breakfast while we enjoyed watching yet another fantastic Southwest sunrise.

Unbeknownst to me, the weather in Wolf Creek Pass, just forty-three miles northwest of Pagosa Springs, was changing dramatically by the minute.

By the time we arrived at the pass an hour later, the roads were already snow-packed. Even though I was driving a four-wheel-drive vehicle, that alone didn't ensure complete safety or success when negotiating the pass. I had driven the pass on numerous occasions but only once in a snowstorm.

The low-hanging clouds were halfway down the thirteen-thousand-foot peaks that surround Wolf Creek pass. This was a valid sign that told me by the time we got to the summit, we could be driving in a blinding blizzard. If this storm was as bad as it appeared to be, we might not even make the summit. If we did make the summit and the storm was widespread, we might not make down the other side.

As I pulled off the road, Cindy asked me what I was going to do. I told her what our options were and that I felt certain we were on the outer edge of a blizzard. She agreed. I closed my eyes and was reminded of a situation in Farmington where Cindy and I had witnessed Sherry Sprinkle making it snow on a cloudless night when the sky was studded with stars. I wished she was here now. With my eyes still closed, I visualized beautiful sunny blue skies over Wolf Creek Pass. I asked God to grant everyone safe passage this day.

I exhaled deeply and opened my eyes. I glanced over at Cindy and she was smiling. "You are going to move this storm, aren't you? Just like Sherry made it snow that night in Farmington, you're going make this snow go bye-bye, huh?"

"Well," I said, "I have been practicing using my projected thought energy to make clouds disappear, so I figured, why not at least try to move this storm out of our way?" At that exact moment, the sun started to break through the cloud formation to the north of our location.

Cindy grabbed my hand and said, "Look, look over there! The sun is beginning to come out from behind the clouds."

I closed my eyes once again in thanks. I had an attitude of gratitude.

I put the vehicle in drive and started up the mountain. By the time we reached the summit, we were rewarded with blue sunny skies that lasted the entire ten days we were in Colorado.

During our ten-day stay, Cindy found the house of her dreams, I located a lender, and we closed on the house before we left town. Doors and windows were flying open like I had never seen before. I knew in my heart of hearts Colorado was where we were destined to be. I never questioned why.

I was certain the *why* would be revealed to me in the near future. When we got back to Farmington, Cindy contacted Ted and Sherry to tell them about all the good stuff that had happened while we were in Colorado.

As would be expected, Sherry was exuberant about our good fortune. She also wanted to know if we would be interested in spending New Year's Eve with them and Mary Ross. She said Ted was all excited about bringing in the New Year with all of their friends present and accounted for. She also reminded Cindy to remind me about getting a spiritual reading from Mary.

Cindy accepted the invitation to the New Year's Eve celebration and told Sherry she would remind me to get the reading from Mary. That evening over supper, Cindy told me about the New Year's Eve party and reminded me to get a reading from Mary. I remember replying, "That's right. I need to put that on my must-do list first thing in the morning. Thanks for the reminder!"

She retorted, "You really need to get that done. It's important!"

I got up from the table and offhandedly stated, "I know. I promise before I leave for Colorado I will get the reading." I went downstairs to my office and made some phone calls. Afterward I sat daydreaming about the future. Everything was unfolding so quickly and smoothly I didn't see any need to get a reading. Besides, what if this Mary person told me not to go to Colorado, like Ja-Zon had advised me not to go to Boise, Idaho? At this point, I didn't want to risk knowing that.

All of a sudden, an image of my brother came to mind. I had not seen or spoken to him in years. I heard he was somewhere in northern California.

Eureka, California sounded familiar. I dismissed the thought and started to busy myself with more pertinent stuff. Instead the thought of "Call your brother, get in touch with your brother Bill now" kept coming to mind. I couldn't shake the notion, so I called Information. They had no listing, so I called my mother in hopes she would have a contact number for him. As all moms do, she did. And of course she wanted to know why I wanted to get in touch with Bill. I said I didn't know and I just had a feeling come over me that I should get in touch with him. At that point mom perked right up. "Do you think something is wrong?" I responded with, "No, it's not that kind of feeling, Mom! I just need to talk to him. I don't know why." Fortunately she let it go at that. I thanked her for the information and then we hung up.

I called his contact number and left a message for Bill to call me back at his leisure. Normally I wouldn't have expected him to call me back, but in my gut I knew he would.

Don't get me wrong; I loved my older brother, but most of his life had been filled with such extraordinary pain and suffering that it was very difficult to stand back, watch, and not judge or criticize his motives

My only salvation was in realizing it was his life to live. His choices had to be his responsibility. It was a bitter pill for me to swallow because he could have been anything he wanted to be.

Bill's capacity to understand complex information was unlimited. In high school he never had to bring work home because he had a photographic memory. He was so extraordinary as a child my folks were told to have his IQ tested. The test came back ranking him in the genius category, 163. It is sad he spent his early years being bored and unchallenged.

His natural musical ability was very impressive too. His singing voice, although undeveloped, was a very rich tenor. He taught himself how to play piano, bass, lead, and rhythm guitar. Additionally he played trumpet and drums.

He was also blessed with an athletic body, and to top it off, he was movie-star handsome. Bill had it all, and though his choices and actions were always questionable, he was always courageous about the results.

He never flinched when it came to taking the consequences of his actions. It was like he had chosen to experience life on his own terms and was prepared to pay a heavy toll along the way, knowing it was to be his destiny. It was heartbreaking to watch.

If Bill lacked anything, it was wisdom, discipline, and self-respect. Only he would have known what he saw when he looked at his reflection in a mirror.

He battled alcoholism his entire adult life. This in itself diminished his life force, affecting his emotional, physical, and intellectual capacities.

However, in 1980, Bill was in a state of sobriety. His personal and financial success was obvious. He owned and maintained a fleet of taxi cabs. He managed his drivers very professionally. As you might recall, I mentioned in chapter one, I worked for Bill for a limited time. It was the only time in my life that I remembered he was sober for any length of time.

The best I can recall, Bill fell off the wagon in 1983 and never recovered. The price was heavy. He lost his business, home, and his family. We never discussed it, but I believe he just gave up. He became a flea-market person. He bought stuff cheap and then sold his goods at flea markets. In 1995, this choice almost cost him his life.

An unknown assailant hit him from behind, knocking him unconscious. While he was down the assailant proceeded to kick him in the face, smashing all his facial bones in the process. The doctors were able to save his life by putting his face back together with metal plates and screws, but he left the hospital terribly disfigured.

I heard he had no place to go, so I drove to Fort Worth, Texas and put him up in a reasonably priced hotel room for six months. I thought he should focus on healing and not have to worry about room and board. My understanding was that once he mended he couldn't take the Texas heat and moved to northern California. I think he chose to be around people who wouldn't ask him a bunch of questions.

In the late 1990s, the family celebrated several marriages and mourned several deaths. Bill always showed up for these occasions, and then he would disappear again. Since his divorce and physical beating, he was not the same man. I wasn't either.

Anyway, the following morning I received a call from Bill. I told him I had recently received a promotion and that Cindy and I were moving to Colorado.

I explained the house we had bought was very large and had plenty of room, just in case he had any desire to move away from California. He said my timing was incredible. He had just been thinking about leaving a couple of days before. He just didn't have anywhere to go or transportation to get there. I suggested he sell what he could over the next week or so, give the rest away, and then get on a bus to Farmington. I informed him that I would be leaving for Colorado on the fifth of January. He asked how Cindy felt about all this. I told him she was very excited about the entire situation. I explained that I had to be in Colorado no later than the sixth of January and that Cindy would meet us in Colorado in mid to late January. So we would have to rough it till Cindy arrived.

I thought I heard real excitement in his voice when he said, "This sounds like a real adventure. I really appreciate you thinking about me." I told him that although I had not called before, it didn't mean that in the past I hadn't thought about him or wondered how he had been doing. I earnestly told him we were very excited about him moving to Colorado with us. I reminded him that our sister Kristen and her family, Kevin Jr. and his family, Tonya and her family, and our mother were already living in Bailey and parts of Denver. "Ya know, it'll be like a family reunion!" I stated. He agreed. He told me he would call me and let me know what bus he would be on and its arrival time. I told him I would be looking forward to his call. It would be three days later he called and five days after that he arrived in Farmington.

In between the last phone call I received from Bill and the day he arrived, I finished up all the packing I needed to get done for trip. Cindy and I had also thoroughly enjoyed bringing in the New Year with Ted, Sherry, and Mary.

Yes, it's true; Mary Ross (the dark-haired woman) and Kevin McPeek, Sr. finally crossed paths. I wish I could tell you at this point in the story I had recognized who Mary really was, but I didn't. I mean I knew she was a very powerful spiritual reader. I just was not aware she was the dark-haired woman whom Ja-Zon had forecasted nearly two years earlier would show up in Farmington before I left. Meeting Mary Ross was special.

As we slow-danced across the floor, Mary's facial expressions took on an angelic glow that went beyond being happy, peaceful, or contented. It was as if I was holding a human being in my arms that had been in the presence of God and now reflected his essence. Her voice was very soft yet crisp whenever she spoke. Her laughter was pleasant. I guess I don't need to tell you, but I will: her hair was somewhat long, straight, and defiantly jet black.

I listened as she conversed with Cindy and the others in our group. Her conversations were lively, lighthearted, and delightfully harmonious. I noticed she squinted a lot, almost like a person who should be wearing glasses but for whatever reason doesn't. I questioned her about it and she told me that she was able to see human auras. I then asked about auras.

She explained to me that all human beings have a luminous radiation that surrounds their physical bodies. She explained further that each aura has a very distinct shape and individual color scheme depending on what a person is thinking or feeling in the moment. If their mood changes, so will the shape and color of an aura. Although I had never seen anyone's aura, I was fascinated Mary was able to. With over two hundred couples milling around, it was no wonder she was squinting. She must have been seeing a kaleidoscope of color.

After bringing in the New Year of 2002, Ted, Sherry, Mary, Cindy, and I walked out to the parking lot, exchanging hugs. I looked skyward, noticing the stars were out in mass. No wonder it was so darn crisp and cold. Sadness gripped me knowing I would be leaving for Colorado in five days. As we exchanged goodbyes, I realized this would most likely be our final hoorah.

In that fleeting moment, I figured out the reason I had spent my lifetime saying goodbye to the people I have loved the most, past and present.

We all have lessons to learn from others or lessons to teach to others.

Once those lessons are learned or taught, we move on in order to continue our personal or spiritual growth. For those of us who are not as nomadic as others, we may not move as much or at all. But new people will always show up to teach us or learn from us. It is what relationship-building is all about.

It is what our true reality is.

They say hindsight is twenty-twenty. So in retrospect I can see clearly now that if certain special people in my life had not been inspired to nudge me along, I might not be sitting here allowing God to write this book through me. I am thankful every day for them and the opportunity they afforded to me.

Because of their unwavering faith, I would consciously awaken to my true reality in becoming a creative instrument for God's expression.

Chapter 19
Bill Arrives from California

When Bill got off the bus, I was shocked to see how bad off he was. He hardly had the strength to get himself down the stairs of the bus. I walked over to him and gave him a big bear hug. I placed my hands on his shoulders while stepping back at arms length. Looking him directly in the eye, I asked, "Did you have a tough trip?"

He smiled, wincing a bit, "Yeah, three days on a bus is not my cup of tea!"

"You mean it's not your typical shot of Jack Daniels, don't you?" I smiled back.

He laughed. "I Can't afford the good stuff anymore, Kev!"

While we talked the bus driver unloaded his baggage. I grabbed some of his stuff and headed toward my truck. I was on my way back for a second trip when I noticed him taking a big swig from a paper bag. It was a sure sign he was drinking heavily. I got the rest of his stuff on the second trip. He finally made it to the truck. It was hard for me to watch him shuffling along instead of walking at a normal pace. He had just turned fifty-four on December 3. The life he had been living was taking its toll in a very dramatic way.

I asked him how much alcohol he had been drinking daily. I was astounded by his casual reply. "Last time I measured, it was a little over a half gallon of rock gut whiskey a day."

I responded as nonchalantly as I could, "So what you're telling me is this rotgut whiskey you're drinking is the pain-stopping, put-you-in-the-grave-early kind of whiskey, and not the sipping kind!"

This time I gotta a belly laugh out of him. "Kev, I've never heard anyone describe rotgut whiskey any prettier than that. Oh my. It tastes like kerosene, so I wouldn't recommend sipping it. I drink it only for medicinal purposes." He removed the cap from the bottle inside the paper bag and took another big swig.

I could tell from the just the smell he wasn't kidding; it was rotgut whiskey. "I can tell you this, my brother. You may use that stuff for only medicinal purposes, but I'd be afraid to put it on a surface cut. I'd be scared to death the cut would get infected."

He was laughing so hard as we drove up the back driveway I thought the whiskey in his mouth was going to either go up his nose or all over the glove compartment. Fortunately Bill got his composure back as we pulled up to the back deck. "Man, I haven't laughed this hard since the last time I saw you at Mickey's funeral in Milwaukee, remember?"

As I was getting out of the truck I commented, "Yeah, I remember. A bunch of us were eating a fantastic pizza at that hole-in-the-wall pizza place when Omar and Tim went into their routine."

"Yeah," Bill replied. "They had the entire restaurant in stitches, remember?"

Laughing out loud, I replied, "How could I forget!"

It was with his bags in hand, as we shuffled side by side toward the front door of my house, that I realized how much I had missed my older brother.

Perhaps I was directed to contact Bill because he was so weak and sick.

Maybe he came to stay with Cindy and me because soul to soul he knew I would not be as judgmental about his drinking as I had been in the past. It was all a mystery to me. I just knew that I was happy to see him and very grateful he made the trip.

When we entered the front door, Cindy was waiting. She gave Bill a big hug and told him how glad she was to see him. They exchanged niceties and then she asked if he was hungry. He said he couldn't remember the last time he had eaten a home-cooked meal. I remembered, in the old days when Bill would go on drinking binges, he might not eat for a week. If he hadn't been eating, it was no wonder that he didn't have any strength.

We were all standing in an area between the dining room and the kitchen.

The guest bedroom was located across from where we were standing. I invited Bill to sit down at the dining-room table while I put his luggage in his room. He agreed. I could tell he was wiped out from the trip. I picked up his bags and carried them into the bedroom.

The room was furnished with a queen-size bed. The oversized headboard had lots of shelving and was tucked partially into the old closet area, giving the person laying there a wonderful feeling of seclusion.

Across the room were the vanity, shower, dressing area, linen closet, and a hideaway door that housed the commode. Right next to the bed was the new walk-in closet. Across from the closet was a built-in full-size television that was connected to the satellite dish.

On one side of the bed was a wood-burning fireplace. On the opposite side of the bed was a two-step landing area made of marble that led to the double french doors that opened on to the top deck, which overlooked the glade. My hope was Bill might find his surroundings comfortable for the next few days, before we had to leave for Colorado.

Cindy Persists

The next few days are kind of hazy to me. I do remember, even though Bill was drinking a lot, he seemed to be cutting back some and eating three good solid meals a day. Every day he looked better, and it appeared to me as if he was getting stronger.

The morning of January 4, Cindy found me in the garage finishing loading up the 740IL BMW. Bill and I would be leaving early the next morning, so like normal for me, I was leaving nothing to chance. The car was gassed up; all fluid levels had been checked along with tire pressure, and so on and so forth. I had just put the last piece of luggage in the trunk and was closing the lid when I saw Cindy standing next to the passenger door. I couldn't tell if she was sad or a little irritated.

"What's up?" I asked as innocently as I could.

"I thought you were going to contact Mary Ross for a reading" was all she said.

"To be perfectly honest with you, honey, I don't think I need a reading," I said.

She smiled a knowing smile, stating that I had promised. For the life of me I couldn't understand her persistence. "You're right. I promised both you and Sherry I would get this reading before I left Farmington. I will go upstairs right now and see if Mary is available sometime today," I sweetly replied.

She gave me a long hug and said, "It's really important!"

All I said was "It must be."

Mary answered on the first ring. I cleared my voice as she said, "Hello."

"Hi, Mary, it's Kevin McPeek," I stated clearly.

"Kevin, how are you?" she replied.

"I am really good. Thank you for asking. Mary, I know this is a really short notice, but I was wondering if you would be available sometime today to give me a reading. I am leaving town tomorrow morning for Colorado," I stated boldly.

There was a slight pause and them Mary responded, "Kevin, I don't know if I can today. This is the last day my son is in town." Again there was a slight pause. "Can I call you right back?" she stated.

I was caught off guard a little but responded with, "Yeah, absolutely. And thanks!"

I was in the kitchen waiting on Mary's call back when Bill came strolling out of his room. Smiling, he said, "Are we ready to head out in the morning?"

Somewhat distracted, I muttered, "Yeah, everything's loaded and ready to go!"

A thought flashed before my eyes. "Hey, Bill, have you ever had a spiritual reading?"

Smiling ear to ear, he stated, "Naw, but I have had a couple of out-of-body experiences."

Laughing now, I responded, "Were you sober at the time?"

He looked at me a little weird and said, "Yeah, a matter of fact I was!"

"Really?" I asked.

"Cross my heart hope to die if I tell a lie" was all he said.

"If I pay for your reading, will you get one?" I asked. "I don't know, Kev. That stuff kind of freaks me out. You know what I mean?" he asked.

"Not really. It's actually pretty cool," I said, trying to sound convincing.

The phone rang. It was Mary Ross. She said she would be happy to come over and give me a reading. I was delighted. She said she was leaving now and would be there shortly. I thanked her accordingly.

Ten minutes later Mary was at the front door. Cindy welcomed her in.

After a few minutes of small talk, Mary and I went downstairs to an area in the house where I knew we would not be disturbed.

Before my reading began, I asked Mary if she would give my brother Bill a reading too. She very sweetly explained that her readings were normally three hours long and covered all aspects of human life. She further explained that this process was very demanding on her physiology. I naturally persisted, attempting to negotiate an hour and a half for Bill and an hour and a half for me! Mary then asked if Bill wanted the reading or if I wanted the reading for Bill. I told her the truth. She then told me to ask Bill if he wanted a reading. If he did, she would give him one.

I excitedly excused myself and went looking for Bill. I found him in the guest bedroom. "Guess what? Mary said she would give you a reading, but there is a catch," I stated quietly.

Bill looked up from the book he was reading, "What's the catch?"

Grinning, I said, "You have to tell me you want a reading!"

He frowned a bit, telling me he had already told me that psychics freak him out.

"C'mon," I urged him. "You may never get another chance like this again!"

I felt like he was giving it some thought as he sat up on the edge of the bed. "Okay, tell Mary I want a reading from her!"

I winked at him, tickled that I had been able to coax him just a little. "I'll come back to get you when I am finished." As I was going back downstairs, I wondered if I should have told him the reading would take three hours.

The Rainbow Connection

I want to remind the reader that even at this stage of my awareness I didn't know Mary was the dark-haired woman Ja-Zon had told me about two years prior to this actual meeting. I also want to mention the reading I am about to summarize is just that—a summary. I will attempt to highlight what I feel is pertinent at this time.

Like Ja-Zon's, Mary's reading was recorded. I would also like to add that it was not my idea to record these readings. I would never have had the foresight to do so. I am thankful Ja-Zon and Mary did. I have listened to and benefited from these recordings countless times. The recordings have been instrumental in my ability to recall with great accuracy what actually transpired.

Mary began the reading with a lovely prayer. She asked God for his personal guidance in assuring that the information she was about to share with me was accurate and all-knowing. As she began, I noticed she didn't have any tarot cards. I wondered why but I didn't ask.

Mary explained in great detail that people were spiritual beings having human experiences, stating that each soul had its own capacity and was its own unique individual expression of God. She explained further that Earth was like a school and that as a soul evolved, its human counterpart always awakened to its true reality. This act of awakening always occurs when a person is in the process of living his or her last lifetime as a human being.

Mary stated that we are conditioned to look outside of ourselves when we are looking for answers to our problems, when in actuality the answers to our issues are always found inside ourselves. She explained that most of us are so involved with the physical world, attempting to fulfill ourselves with material gains and various physical relationships, and so busy with our individual attachments that the information we are looking for remains dormant.

Mary then purported that the universe we live in is neutral. "What we perceive as good and bad, rich or poor is a human phenomenon. This human conditioning is firmly established and takes center stage as we move from childhood into adulthood. Those belief systems make us petty, judgmental, untrusting, fearful, and disruptive. We learn early on as we mature not to take risks, venture out, think beyond normal guidelines, or take action that could be perceived as questionable," she stated, "Parents want children who fit in, who are thought to be normal, and who represent them well."

Mary continued, "The challenge this creates is that every child born on planet Earth has a different capacity and is a unique expression of God's love. In most instances our human belief systems stifle their spiritual experiences. If this occurs they will not learn the lessons they came here to learn, and therefore they will have to make another trip, back to Earth."

As I pondered Mary's words, I couldn't help but reflect on my own life. I had spent most of my time attempting to fit in, while at the same time knowing life had to have a greater purpose. Although I had had many successes in my life, I had certainly experienced just as many failures. Whether up or down, I had always looked for the essence of truth, attempting to find the reason why some things worked while others didn't. Looking inside was always painful. It was always easier to search outside of myself for illumination.

Listening to Mary, I now realized how small I had been and how confining my belief systems were. Simultaneously I became aware of a great capacity I had not tapped into. I knew that if what Mary was saying was true, then I too, like everyone else, was a unique expression of God's love. The power was inside of me, not outside of me. I just needed to have the courage and discipline to go there.

Mary continued; "Everything we think comes from either thoughts of fear or love. Thoughts are things. The ego has its own agenda. In the state of being self-centered, one becomes self-absorbed. This lifestyle feeds the ego. When one becomes consciously awake to their higher nature, they very naturally begin to filter information using the gift of their emotions, and not their egos." Mary explained to me that when I was feeling good, what I was actually feeling was God's love. When I was feeling bad, I was actually feeling some form of fear-based belief system, which made me feel separated from God. When I felt upset, angry, resentful, revengeful, or judgmental, those feelings were signals that I was allowing my ego to filter information rather than my higher nature.

Mary further explained that this dualistic nature that all human beings have is in a constant state of influx as humans attempt to map and remap the world in which they choose to live. Becoming aware of how I filtered and processed my thoughts according to how I felt would determine which method I used to assist myself in creating my own personal reality. She explained that no matter what kind of chaos or suffering was going on around me, I could consciously choose to trust in God's love, having faith that the past, present, and future are as they should be. If my thoughts were fear-based, I should be aware that I was allowing my ego to filter my experience. When I learned to be responsible in the moment whenever conflicts from within or outside myself appeared on the horizon, my thoughts would begin to transcend themselves, allowing me the freedom to take the information I was being given and either apply it or discard it, without reacting to it in a negative way.

Mary went on to state the true purpose for our meeting was that although I had been a true seeker all my life, I was at a critical point in my spiritual evolution. On a higher level of conscious awareness, the request was that I learn to shift my thinking in order to fulfill my life's purpose. Mary stated her job was to help me connect to the freedom of knowing what was real for me, where I was going, and how I got to where I was.

Mary stated I had been driven in mastering the things outside of myself. I had the natural ability to lead people. She said that this ability to lead others had been earned in other lifetimes. She stated clearly that I would not have been given this ability or afforded the opportunities to effect souls with any larger influence unless I had earned that right. She then smiled, adding that I had not only earned that right, but had been asked to lead and teach others; stating that was why I was a natural at doing both.

"This is the reason why people have always come to you for advice and counsel. They've known that soul to soul you would have the insights that they needed to assist them in their lives. Under the guise of a normal business setting, you have always been an instrument of truth and counsel," she stated. Smiling again, she commented, "Every person you have encountered in this lifetime has been a perfect interaction, whether you believe it or not. The presence of caring, knowing what others need, sometimes baffles you. You wonder what you are doing with that person, and you won't have a clue. You wonder where the words you have spoken to them come from. You have known just what that person has needed. Bottom line, spirit has been using you to assist those you have helped."

Mary continued, "Your biggest pitfall is your heart is way too compassionate. When you give advice, you are stepping over a boundary, and you don't want to go there. I see sixty-four emotional tentacles attached to you and the people you have advised. Some of your tentacles are over eighteen years old. Emotional tentacles drain your physical and intellectual bodies. To protect you from future tentacles, continue to provide information to people, but tell them they have the freedom to do with the information as they choose to. You cannot feel any emotional attachment to the information you present to others. To rid yourself of the collection of tentacles you have acquired, visualize the people who you have given advice to; bless and tell them you are letting them go. Then cut each of their tentacles with a pair of golden shears while wishing them well." Mary then added, "In the future it would be wise for you to get off by yourself before you give counsel and ask if you should. Guidance will always be provided for you. You will feel this in your heart center."

At this point Mary asked if I had any questions. I told her I didn't. My head was clear and my mind was sharp. The knowledge Mary was giving to me seemed to answer my questions as she went along. It appeared to me God was directing her to fill in my blank spaces. I had the urge to share this information with others. I didn't know who I would share with or how I would do this, but I felt it would have to be done.

As if being able to read my mind, Mary continued. "You will have to complete your life mastery before you will be ready to share your life experiences with people outside your sphere of influence." She looked at me seriously, affirming she was being directed to be very precise with the timeframes she was about to provide to me. She stated, "These timelines will become very important to you as you move forward. For the next four years they will guide you along your way." She stated that I had a very powerful mind that was capable of taking complicated information, and making it very simple to understand. This ability was one of my many gifts.

Mary paused and then began again. "This year, 2002, you will take the information that is being provided to you this day and continue to build on the information until you develop a solid base of knowledge. You will learn to listen from within while you do outside research in order to expand your unique understanding of spirituality"

Mary continued, "In a year and half to two years from now you, will begin to journal your thoughts and ideas, forming them into powerful concepts. From now until then, you will begin to express your thoughts to the people within your sphere of influence in a very easy-to-understand, lighthearted way. Those you choose to share this information with will be receptive. This information will be a mixture of business ideas based upon human values and spiritual consciousness."

Mary paused again for just a moment but then continued. "Understand the people who you will be responsible for in the near future are ready for you to provide them with very unique ways to enhance not only their business savvy, but their personal lives as well. Patience will serve you well here."

Mary then laughed aloud. "You have such intensity and a seriousness about you that learning the art of staying calm, patient, and lighthearted will serve you well."

Smiling back at her, I replied, "That obvious, huh?"

"Oh yeah, and you carry all your stress in your neck. Even right this minute, the muscles in your neck are like little steel bars!" she reported. "When we get into the health part of the reading, I will tell you how to fix that," she stated.

Mary continued, "Two to three years from now, you will continue to have moments of creative thinking that will astound even you. You be given insights that are able to resolve many of the challenges that you will be facing over the next two- to three-year timeframe Do not hesitate to act on those insights, because although the people you work for may not have the knowledge or foresight to understand your methodology, you will succeed if you act instinctively.

"In 2004, the company you are working for will attempt to shake up your world. Remain steadfast and respond responsibly, because your work will not be finished yet.

"In the mid year of 2005, you will begin to notice a desire to spend more time alone. Your thoughts will start to transcend themselves, providing you with great inspirations. This will be a sign that you are finishing up your life mastery. It will become very obvious to you by October of 2005 that your focus is changing. If you surrender to this calling, you will finish your work with SONIC restaurants very naturally."

Teasingly I asked, "Am I going to get fired?"

Mary chuckled. "They may not understand everything you do, but they do know you are one of the best. They'd like to keep you around for the next twenty years, if they could!"

Mary continued, "If you choose to follow your life plan, in January 2006 you will begin to write books."

I sat there in my living room in a state of shock and awe. Mary had just dropped a two-ton bomb on me and I needed a moment to recover from being shell-shocked. I had no interest in writing even one book, much less several books. I knew my writing and grammar skills were pretty limited. I certainly didn't have the educational training or the slightest expertise to even know how to get started. So I asked, "Mary, are you sure I am supposed to write books in the future?"

She smiled, realizing this would be quite a leap in faith for me to grasp. "You will not only write books, Kevin, but you will become an inspirational speaker as well. You will write books for both adults and children. You will teach businessman how to increase their business holdings without using the cutthroat techniques and greedy tactics currently being used. You will be given insights into how to reach out to children in a fun, lighthearted way that will inspire them to want to read your books. Your message to them will be disguised but effectively clear and precise." She paused and then stated, "You have a lot of work to do!"

I replied, "Yeah, my life isn't going to be over tomorrow, huh?"

She laughed out loud and said, "No you have a lot of work to do!"

Mary quickly began again, "Let's talk for a moment about the law of attraction. The perception most people have pertaining to the law of attraction is it does not exist. They don't want to believe the situations or the people that keep showing up in their world are the people and situations they are personally manifesting through their ability to make decisions based upon their thoughts, ideas, and belief systems. If everything is going well in their world, they give the credit to their egos. If everything is not going well, then they blame God, the devil, or anyone else outside of themselves. If they do look inside themselves when their perception is things are not going well, then their ego takes over their thought process and assists them in creating their mental anguish, emotional suffering, and/or guilt. The truth is we are all bound by the spiritual law of attraction, just as we are bound by the natural law of gravity. It does not matter if you are a good person or a bad person; if you jump off a building, you will certainly hit the ground. The law of attraction, although more subtle and camouflaged, contains the same analogy.

"Your thoughts determine your intent and your intentions will activate the law of attraction, which is neutral, just like the law which governs gravity. It does not matter if your intentions are honorable or not, because once you activate the law of attraction, it will manifest in the material world, unless you change your intention, which will delay or evaporate the manifestation."

I cleared my throat. "I am really glad to know that," I remarked. "For a minute there I had the feeling all my thoughts might manifest themselves!"

Mary smiled patiently, explaining that most people have around sixty thousand thoughts per day. In order to activate the law of attraction for a particular thought, a person had to be consciously aware of that thought, be able to visualize that thought, and put a great deal of human emotion behind that thought in order to activate the law of attraction. She stated most people believe their thoughts are on autopilot, and therefore are unaware that their thoughts can have a powerful impact on their surrounding circumstances.

She said most people didn't understand that they had been given the authority, ordained by God, in the form of free will. This loving act of God gave them dominion over the world that they have created for themselves.

At this point in Mary's reading I had become totally absorbed in what she was saying. In my gut I knew she was speaking the truth because over my lifetime I had experienced most of the information she was exposing me to, but because of my ridged belief systems, I had failed to see but just a few of the possibilities that had always been around me. I hope you (the reader) will pay very close attention to Mary's insights on the next page.

If you will learn to apply this information, it will forever change the way you look at yourself and the world in which you live.

As I looked up, my eyes met Mary's. "I can see your mind is racing a million miles per hour," she stated somewhat cautiously.

Smilingly, I reported, "Yeah, you're filling up my bucket really fast!"

She laughed, "As usual you are underestimating your learning capacity and your natural ability to absorb verbal communications while you process the information in your own unique way."

I thought to myself, *Very nicely stated.* But I secretly wondered how she knew that. I quickly put my mind at ease remembering "that in God, all things were possible." All I had to do was open my mind and allow the information to flow in and not judge or question its value or validity.

Mary began again, "You have a very powerful intellectual mind, Kevin. Because of this you have always known you had the ability to not only create your present moment but also the future as you saw it. In knowing you could do this, you have suffered many logical consequences along the way. These consequences have taught you lessons that have now become the tools you will use in the future, to assist you in leading others." She paused for a moment as if she was listening to someone else speaking. Then she said, "It is really important that I go back and revisit the law of attraction with you, because you need to fully grasp this law in order to practice and then share the attraction with others.

"The secret to understanding and implementing the law of attraction is becoming responsible for your thoughts. Being responsible in that moment you allow the power of your intention to create what is best not only for you, but for everyone. Whether you are being responsible in that moment or not, the universal law of attraction will model what you think you want. We do create our world as a result or consequence in what we are thinking and emotionally visualizing in that moment. But understand there is a time delay that gives us the opportunity to redesign and reevaluate our thoughts."

I told Mary I had never heard of the law of attraction, but I understood the power of visualization. I admitted that most of the time I had tried to do things my way, but as she had pointed out earlier those actions resulted in logical consequences, and some big doses of pain and suffering. Mary suggested that the big doses of pain and suffering were a direct result of my overdeveloped ego. We both laughed, knowing it was true. Mary then restated that the results I experienced in creating my life up till now had been an excellent tool for learning. It was now time to take those learning experiences and apply a new value system in order to improve the results.

"Kevin, if in the moment you chose the most powerful energy source in the universe in order to activate the law of attraction, do you suppose the result would ever make you or anybody else suffer?"

I didn't hesitate, "Probably not."

She smiled knowingly. "The reason you have suffered in the past, creating logical consequences you then would have to deal with, is because, in the moment of creation, your thoughts were fear-based. Fear-based energy represents the lower nature of man. It is driven by the ego/personality. The ego is the main cause of all of mankind's problems because mankind allows the ego to define who we think we are, as individuals, and collectively as separate societies. The ego defines our worthiness according to the kind of clothes we wear, the cars we drive, the houses we live in, our education level, et cetera. When we base our worthiness on our ego, we naturally develop a need for greed. These egotistical thoughts keep us from solving our most basic social problems as well."

At this point I had to jump in. "Mary I understand what you are saying, but I am really anxious to know what the most powerful universal energy is that activates the law of attraction?"

Again Mary smiled, this time a little sheepishly, "Love is the most powerful universal energy," she stated. She then commented, "You look a little disappointed. Were you expecting something a little more complicated or tricky?"

I paused for a moment. "Yeah, I think so" was my response.

Mary chuckled. "I know it sounds way too simple, but it is just that simple. Each of us has the capacity to control our individual thoughts. Each of us can choose how we respond or react to how we feel. The law of attraction will begin to manifest miracles that will keep you in a constant state of awe. The law of attraction activated with love will allow the right people to show up when you need them. It will create the right situations for you to learn from. Your creative imagination will transcend your thoughts and ideas. Your life and those around you will become harmoniously abundant."

Mary paused once again and then continued, "The love God bestows on each of us is unconditional. You don't have to qualify or wait to be anointed."

Mary waited a moment as she let her words soak in, "Although God is impersonal to our human endeavors here on Earth. God watches very closely the spiritual evolution of every human being. All negative connotations such as blame and judgment were put into the system in order to punish, control, and allow human beings to suffer so that the spiritual body could evolve."

Mary could tell I was a little uncomfortable with her summarization of the human existence versus the evolution of the spiritual body, but she continued anyway. "The good news is when a human being consciously awakens to their true reality, in knowing they are spiritual beings having a human experience, they will have mastered their human life and spiritual evolution. The lifetime in which this occurs is always their last lifetime on planet Earth."

Mary began to speak again. "Kevin, the main reason we were supposed to meet this day was to ensure you have awakened to who you really are. Your rainbow connection has been completed. You now know on a conscious level that you are a spiritual being in a human body. You now are aware on a conscious level that you are an eternal being of pure light. What you do with this information is totally up to you. If you expand your essence, seeking your own truth, your life will become very calm, filled with contentment. You will touch the lives of countless others. If you decide over the next four years to stay on your current path, God will continue to bless your ability to touch the lives of others in a very positive way, but your reach will be severely restricted to your sphere of influence. Either path will be honored universally. Your gifts and insights are uniquely yours to share any way you choose to."

Mary then reached out and took my hand, stating in a very loving way, "In the future when you apply the law of attraction, be responsible in the moment. Connect with God's love and leave your ego behind. Ask for guidance in everything you do. As you expand your knowledge and increase your faith, you will no longer be bound by the restraints of the physical material world."

She smiled while gently squeezing my hand and said, "Miracles big and small will abound."

I realized in that moment that all human beings were actually spiritual beings having human experiences. I recognized that the cabdriver I had met twenty-two years ago had been a highly evolved spiritual being, disguised as a cabdriver, whom God had sent to me in an attempt to welcome me into his metaphysical world. And even though I had not been ready to accept his offer at that time, I now was. I knew the information I had been given since then had been carefully crafted not only in content, but in the timing of it as well. I didn't totally understand everything Mary had shared with me, but I did know that this information needed to be treated seriously and with a great deal of care. And although my patience and actions over the next four years waned from time to time, becoming aware of my conscious thought processes assisted greatly in what I was able to attract into my life and share with other people.

Mary finished my reading by explaining to me any health-related concerns or weaknesses she thought I should be aware of. The information Mary provided allowed me to avoid a major heart attack in April 2004, repair my digestive system, and be open to finding and practicing a breathing technique called Qigong (pronounced "chee-gong"). Qigong is an easy-to-follow healing method based on ancient Chinese practices that were closely guarded for thousands of years. Qigong exercises release blockages and restores health using the body's energy called "Qi." This system delivers vibrancy, and a feeling of well being. Master Chunyi Lin's Qigong has assisted many people who suffer breathing problems.

The health portion of the reading completed my reading. I looked at my watch and exactly three hours had passed. I was amazed at how quickly the time had passed. It was now Bill's turn for his reading. Three hours later she and Bill were finished.

Mary had recorded his reading too. I was somewhat surprised that Bill wanted me to listen to his reading, because he was a very private person. To know Bill was to only know what Bill wanted you to know.

I found out Bill was very interested in the Akashic Records. At the time of our readings, I had no knowledge of what the Akashic Records were, but he knew. If you don't know what the Akashic Records are or why they are kept, I will explain the best I can.

The *akashic* is a Sanskrit word meaning "space," "sky," or "ether." The information contained in the records is a collection of mystical knowledge that is stored on a non-physical plane of existence. The Akashic Records have existed since creation. Contained in the records are human, animal, plant, and mineral events and responses concerning consciousness in all realities. A physical medium can become a "witness" and achieve preconscious access to the records. While in the Akashic Records, a witness can view both the past events and responses of an individual.

Karma is also revealed. Stated simply, a physical medium can view a person's past lifetimes. Many psychics have this ability, as does Mary.

As I listened to Bill's tape recording, it was obvious he wanted information about his past lifetimes. Mary attempted to discourage his request, but he was very persistent. She finally relented. As she opened up the Akashic book containing his past lifetimes, I heard her gasp out loud and then become very silent for a very long moment. I wondered what she had seen that had frightened her so much. Neither Bill nor I would ever get to know.

She began softly, "Bill, please understand it would do you absolutely no good in this lifetime for me to reveal to you information concerning your past lifetimes. What is very positive for you to know is that all the karmic debt that you created in past lifetimes has been paid back in this lifetime. You finished paying back this karma about six months ago. I must tell you I have never seen anyone that God has allowed to take on so much karmic debt in one lifetime. You have a very powerful, persuasive soul that basically convinced God that your God self had the capacity to accomplish this in just one human lifetime." She paused for just a moment and then continued. "You have a very strong physical constitution that has served you very well in getting this done. Even though your spiritual self has driven your physical self to the brink on numerous occasions, the physical you has served its purpose well. Understand this is why your current life has been so difficult."

Again she slightly paused, perhaps waiting for the proper phrasing of her next sentence. "Bill, the good news is you are now free to finish out this lifetime as you choose."

The rest of Bill's reading I decline to make public. All spiritual readings are quite enlightening and quite personal. I will, however, comment that after listening to Bill's entire reading, I realized that although on the surface his life appeared disruptive and destructive, the underbelly of his existence was his true reality. And although many had tried to influence his life in a positive way, Bill had always rejected their influences in order to stay the course. I learned that all I could do was love Bill unconditionally.

I suggest to the reader, if you haven't received a spiritual reading, develop the courage do so. Most of us have an inner desire to do this, but our human fear keeps us from actually doing it. I dare you to become bigger and better by gaining the knowledge that is available to you.

Chapter 20
Snow, Ghosts, and a Revelation

Bill and I arrived in Monument, Colorado on the fifth of January, 2002. After shoveling and de-icing the severely sloping sixty-six-foot-long and twelve-foot-wide driveway, we then had to contend with shoveling the snow off the 1,500-square-foot parking area before we were able to drive my car into the garage. I decided that if I couldn't find some kid or local company to shovel my driveway, I would have to purchase a four-wheel-drive vehicle that was capable of traversing this treacherous driveway.

I gave Bill a tour of the house, deciding along the way which bedrooms we wanted. Bill chose a bedroom downstairs and I of course took the master bedroom upstairs. After we unloaded the car and put our meager belongings away, we then assisted each other blowing up our individual airbeds. After we had finished, we went to the kitchen to fix dinner. As I was scrambling some eggs, Bill said, "This house is kind of creepy with nothing in it." I laughed while nodding my head in agreement. "I am being serious, Kev. I don't want to offend you, but this house is really spooky!"

Trying to be dead serious, I told him he was just tired and hungry. "Most likely we are going to hear the crackle of the walls and the squeaking of the floors for the next two weeks until Cindy arrives with the furniture." I suggested he get used to it.

After we were through eating, I made some necessary phone calls and then got ready for bed. Just as I was about to turn the lamp off, I heard Bill walking down the hallway and into my room. Before I could turn over to see what he needed, I heard him turn around and walk back down the hallway. I called out to him, but he was already gone. I turned off the light and slept heavily that first night.

When I awoke the next morning, Bill was already up fixing breakfast. "How did you sleep last night?" I asked.

"Not very well," he shot back at me. "How about you?" he asked.

"As they say, I slept like a log," I countered. "You mean to say you didn't hear any of the commotion that was going on in the kitchen last night? It sounded like you were up here slamming the cupboard doors and flinging food around. I came up to check it out, but nothing was out of place!"

"What time was that?" I asked,

"It was exactly 3:00 a.m.," he stated emphatically!

"Like I said, I slept very soundly last night. I didn't hear anything unusual," I reported.

"Well, what I heard last night wasn't the walls crackling or the floors squeaking; that's for sure!" he again emphatically stated.

I thought for a moment and then asked, "So what did you need last night?"

"When last night," he asked?

"I guess it was around eleven when I heard you come down the hall and into my room, but before I could turn over you had already left," I stated.

Excitedly he responded, "You see now. I told you this house is spooky. We've got some ghosts hanging around. I didn't come back upstairs until three in the morning!"

I didn't want to feed his imagination anymore than was necessary, so I just let it go at that, but I had an eerie feeling we weren't alone in this house.

The third night I awoke at exactly at 3:00 a.m. I immediately sat straight up and slowly glanced around the darkened room. A wonderful feeling of peace surrounded me. As I slowly gained consciousness, my thoughts began to focus on Mary. I realized in that quiet moment of recollection that Mary had been the dark-haired woman I was to meet before I left Farmington. I remember wanting to get up and dance around my bedroom, feeling giddy, foolish, and softly laughing aloud, my mind flashed an image of Ebenezer Scrooge and how he felt the morning after he had spent Christmas Eve with his three spirit guides.

Instead of getting up and dancing around the darkened bedroom, I picked up my cell phone and called the only person on the planet who would not only want to share in this revelation but might be able to confirm it as well.

You guessed correctly. I was calling my lovely wife, Cindy.

As the phone began to ring, I felt a moment of guilt, believing I was being a bit selfish in waking her up just so she could settle me down.

I dare say a bigger and better man would have had the self-control to wait until a reasonable hour in which to share his information. I was about to hang up when she answered, "Hi, honey, is anything wrong?"

"No, everything is fine," I reported back to her. "I just wanted to share a revelation with you that I just had, and hopefully you can confirm it!"

There was a moment of silence and then she said, "Of course, I will try to do my best. What was revealed to you?"

Trying to contain the excitement in my voice, I paused for what seemed an eternity before I spoke again. "Do you remember almost two years ago when we went to Ja-Zon for information regarding Boise, Idaho?"

"Of course," she stated with a smile in her voice. "You were directed by Ja-Zon and her guides to not leave Farmington until you met a dark-haired woman. If you chose to leave before your meeting with her, the rainbow which would benefit many would not get connected."

My jaw dropped, "You are good!" I stated emphatically.

"Thanks," she quickly replied.

"You probably know about my revelation too, huh," I asked jokingly.

"What, that Mary was the dark-haired woman?" she asked.

I faltered for the right words. "Yeah, I had apparently forgotten almost everything Ja-Zon had told me. It wasn't till just a few minutes ago that everything came flooding back to me, connecting all the dots. Mary was the dark-haired woman I was supposed to meet," I said softly as a tear fell from my cheek.

Again there was a long pause, and then I heard Cindy's comforting voice say, "Kev, you have been so physically busy the past forty-five days you were totally oblivious that this was going on around you. The forces beyond your human awareness had to come together to ensure your meeting with Mary had taken place before you left Farmington. It was important!"

All I could muster in response was a muffled, "Thank you."

We exchanged the words *I love you* and then disconnected our call. I got up and located my micro cassette recorder. I went back to bed turned on the recorder and listened to Mary's entire reading. I laid there thankful that her words had been recorded. I made a promise to myself that I would not forget Mary's words like I had Ja-Zon's. I would never become so busy physically that I would allow myself to become oblivious to what was going on around me in a spiritual sense. It has been almost five years now, and I have not broken either of these promises. As promised to me by Mary, it didn't take long for both small and large miracles to begin showing up in an abundant way.

Living without Cindy

The next eleven days without Cindy were, to say the least, interesting. I would leave for work early in the morning and return late in the evening.

I had bought Bill some books and a flat-screen television, which was hooked up to the satellite dish to help keep him entertained while I was gone.

He loved the History, Discover, and National Geographic channels. At night when I'd get home, he could hardly wait to tell me about all the stuff he'd watched during the day.

We would always meet in the kitchen, and while I cooked dinner I'd listen to him recount the information he had gathered throughout the day. He did a great job keeping me up to date on current events as well as local news.

When dinner was ready, we would pull out our folding chairs and gather around the rather large carton the television came in, which now served as our dining-room table as well. Bill would crank up the fireplace while I finished putting all the goodies on the table box. After dinner Bill would clean up the kitchen and wash the dishes while I made my phone calls.

I noticed Bill's drinking had subsided greatly. His physical strength and stamina improved daily. His bouts of depression seemed to be diminishing.

It became a ritual that nightly before we went to bed, we would sit in the lotus position in front of the fireplace while meditating. I awoke one morning flat on my back but still in the cross-legged lotus position. Although I had trouble uncrossing my legs, it was honestly one of the best nights of sound sleep I had experienced in years. The two weeks Bill and I spent together, just the two of us, will always remain as very special memories for me.

CINDY ARRIVES

Except for the first night we spent in the house, our entity didn't bother us again until after Cindy arrived. Lights that worked fine started to not work at all, and then just as suddenly they would work again just fine. Our animals would be inside the house when we left and would be outside when we returned home a few hours later. Or they would be outside when we left and inside when we arrived home again.

One night Bill stated he heard Cindy knocking on his bedroom door, telling him it was time to get up. When he opened the door, nobody was there. He looked at the clock and again it was three o'clock in the morning.

Cindy and I continued to hear someone occasionally walk down the hallway into our bedroom, stop, turnaround, and walk back down the hallway. It reminded us of perhaps a parent who was checking on his or her children.

Bill, Cindy, and I didn't feel threatened by any of these strange occurrences. However, if there was a spirit trapped in between dimensions, we felt an obligation to try to help it crossover. After gathering some information, it became a simple process. Bill volunteered to be the one to explain very nicely to this entity that he or she was dead and should go to the light. Since then we have never felt the presence of this particular entity.

For those doubting Thomases out there who have not had the opportunity to make contact with a trapped spirit, ghost, or entity, I understand your dilemma in lacking the faith to believe that these phenomena exist, as do your guides and your angels, who attempt to provide you with guidance and protection. Remember, at one time I was a doubting Thomas too.

As you allow your human consciousness to acknowledge the fact that you are actually a spiritual being having a human experience, you will have found one of the keys that will unlock one of the many doors to a knowledge that has remained outside your grasp till now, hidden behind the door of your human fear of the unknown and the unexplainable.

The ability to reason is one of our greatest human attributes. It can also be our Achilles heel. I dare you to become bigger and better by reaching out in faith by grasping this secret key in order to unlock the hidden door of knowledge. You will learn that in believing steadfastly, the unknown can be explained and the unexplainable can be known.

When your faith and trust expand beyond that of a mustard seed, you will discover a path for understanding, joyous fulfillment, compassion for the less fortunate, charity for the poor, contentment in doing what is right, love that is boundless, and clarity in all you do.

Bill Begins to Struggle

It took Bill and Cindy less than two weeks to get all the boxes unpacked and the house organized. During this time I contracted to have a dumbwaiter installed, added wood flooring in the laundry room, turned a storage area into a play room for the grandkids, and added five hundred square feet to the existing deck. Since the air in the house was so dry and the water was hard, we also decided to add a humidifier to the heating system and a water-softening system to the water supply.

In addition I was overseeing three supervisors and nineteen restaurants that were spread out as far south as Alamosa to as far north as Longmont, to as far east as Burlington. Most of the other restaurants were located in the Denver metropolis area and the Colorado Springs city limits. The image I am trying to develop here is that Bill, Cindy, the supervisors, and myself were all extremely busy. Once the house was in order, Bill and Cindy were able to relax somewhat, but the supervisors and myself continued to work seven days a week for many months to come.

Most days I would leave early in the morning and wouldn't get home till after eight o'clock at night. I began to notice Bill was drinking a little more each day. When I would arrive home, he would be waiting for me upstairs in the family room, wanting to talk. It was obvious he was struggling with the information Mary had given to him. Because of the amount of alcohol he was consuming daily, he would be argumentative. Our controversial discussions seemed to accomplish nothing. Neither one us ever came to a conclusion that the other could agree with. We just chased each other around in a circle. I think this occurred because I was dead tired and he was loaded.

In mid-February we got a break from each other. Cindy and I had a Merritt convention to attend in Albuquerque, New Mexico. We were gone about four or five days. When we returned, Bill was really hitting the bottle hard.

Every day our relationship appeared to deteriorate more and more. It seemed to me that although Mary had told Bill that his karma had been paid back and he was free to live his life the way he chose to, Bill's choice was to continue being disruptive and destructive. It was heartbreaking to watch.

Toward the end of February, I knew I had to let him go. Trying to protect and care for him was not fair to him or Cindy. It seemed he was to a point where he was feeling a combination of guilt and resentment.

Bill finally decided to leave March 1, 2002 and head back to Fort Worth, Texas. As we were getting ready that morning, our dog of eighteen years went into convulsions and died. "Bear" loved Bill, and it was as if somehow she couldn't stand the thought of him leaving and just gave up. We took Bear to the veterinarian in Monument, and they disposed of her remains. This was very hard on Cindy and me, but it was extremely difficult for Bill. He always had a special love he shared with animals, and the animals always knew it. I asked him if he wanted to delay leaving and he said no.

Bill was scared to death of flying in an airplane, so Cindy and I drove him to the bus station in Colorado Springs.

We hung out with Bill until his bus came in. As he was about to get on the bus, I gave him a hug. Then something came over me and I told him he had a choice; he would have to decide to either continue living in fear or decide to trust God and learn to be of service to others. If he chose to trust God while serving others, his life would be filled with love, hope, and peace. If he chose to live in fear, he wouldn't live more than four more months. He died four months later in July, at age fifty-five years and seven months, from liver failure.

I have often thought if I had kept Bill with me, he might still be alive today.

When that thought enters my conscious awareness, a tiny little voice always states, "Your brother was too tired to change and much older than his human years. Feel no guilt. He suffers no more, so why should you. Be proud your brother stayed the course, and so must you."

Some people believe that humans who think they hear voices are on the verge of needing some professional help. The "super beings" that I know understand these inner thoughts and have learned to trust them.

These voices are your sixth sense, which is referred to as intuition. Intuition is an extremely valuable gift from God. When you become consciously aware of your intuition, intuition will provide you with a guidance system that is foolproof. Included in this system are security and warning devices. We have all had small glimpses of intuition from time to time, but most of us fail to acknowledge the power of our intuition. Intuition is a key that I discovered unleashes a powerful energy that allows me to instantly recognize a potential dangerous situation, a possible threat, or see in my mind's eye a future event unfolding. Human beings refer to intuition as "trusting your gut." When you learn to do this daily, you will open a channel of energy that flows unrestricted between your human self and your God self.

All things then become possible.

Chapter 21
The Rest of the Story

I have always found it interesting that I learn more about myself when I have been defeated or I have failed or have been in a creative struggle than when I have won, or succeeded, or felt I could rest upon my laurels. Perhaps this psychological tiff is normal or perhaps it is a character flaw. Maybe the cliché "learn from your mistakes" is a belief system that I still cling to. With that in mind, I have decided to condense the twenty-first chapter in an effort to highlight my struggles over the next four years while adding, when appropriate, a few sprinkles of wonderment here and there. The rest of the story begins after my brother's death in July of 2002 and ends in January, 2006.

The Year 2002

I had spent from January to July of 2002 working seven days a week. After Bill died I convinced myself I needed someone to metaphysically mentor me.

The restaurants, management teams, and supervisors were all having a banner year as expected, but I personally needed inspiration. I was hungry for more information relating to what I felt would make me a "super being."

In early August I received a phone call from my dad. We talked for a while, discussing pleasantries, and then the phone call turned somewhat ugly. I had brought up a subject that my father was not very fond of: the metaphysical world of spirituality. For sixteen years my dad had been a minister of music at a fundamental Baptist church in Fort Worth, Texas. Even though he had been retired for the past seventeen years, he was still very much involved in the church and religious music.

I was amazed at how low-key I was on the phone. Even though my dad was yelling at me constantly and calling me a cultist, I responded back to him with respect, honor, and love. I attempted to explain to him I had not given up my salvation for spirituality, but he would not hear it. I told him my mind was open and attached to nothing. He stated he believed that my head was empty and no longer attached to my shoulders. He told me he would send me some information relating to cults. He stated sarcastically that if my mind was truly open and attached to nothing, I would find his information enlightening. Throughout our conversation I literally felt the energy in my body draining away. I finally told him I would be happy to look over the information he was sending, and then we disconnected.

As I reflected on our conversation, I couldn't figure out why he had been so angry and mean-spirited. I felt bad, bruised, and deflated. Cindy walked into the kitchen and I recounted my phone call conversation to her.

Sweet as could be, she stated, "What were you expecting?"

Offhandedly I said, "I thought he would at least be civil!"

"Mary warned you about whom to share this information with. Maybe your dad wasn't ready for it!"

I scoffed. "Yeah, no doubt about that!"

I then got up and went downstairs to my small but well-stocked library. I had no idea what I was looking for, but there I was thumbing through every book I had on hand. As I scanned the bookshelf, my eyes fell upon a very thin paperback book entitled *Many Lives, Many Masters*, written by a doctor named Brian L. Weiss. I pulled the book off the shelf and read the front cover,

"The true story of a prominent psychiatrist, his young patient, and the past-life therapy that changed both their lives." I had never seen this book before and was very curious where it had come from. As I thumbed through the pages, I noticed Dr. Weiss had published the book in 1988. The book itself was very worn, but didn't contain any notations or markings.

I ran back upstairs and found Cindy still in the kitchen. A little out of breath, I asked as I laid the book on the counter directly in front of her, "Do you remember unpacking this book?"

She picked up the book and took a very long look at it and then slid it gently back over to me, stating, "Kevin, I have never seen this book before!"

I sat down on one of the wooden bar stools, picked up the book, and fumbled through the first few pages, looking for a table of contents. There wasn't one, just a preface. As I began to read aloud the opening paragraph of the preface Dr. Weiss had written, a chill came over me. "I know that there is a reason for everything. Perhaps at the moment that an event occurs we have neither the insight nor the foresight to comprehend the reason, but with time and patience it will come to light."

I paused for a moment and glanced up at Cindy. The expression on her face said it all. "Looks like you found the book you are supposed to read, huh?" I had neither the insight nor the foresight to explain or comprehend where this book had come from, but I knew the reason I now possessed it. The information that Dr. Weiss was kind enough to share with the world would not only quell the doubts my father had raised, but his story would solidify and magnify my thirst for more information about a world that so few of us have ever even dared to imagine, much less make real.

Still looking at Cindy, I replied, "You and I both know Dr. Weiss is right. There has to be a reason or a purpose for everything that happens to each of us, no matter what our perception is of that event. *Coincidental* is a word I will never use again in this lifetime. To answer your question, this is the book I was destined to read!"

And read it I did—over and over, again and again and again, each time discovering and uncovering other keys to yet other secrets so carefully crafted that only those who were ready and open to receive the information would be able to appreciate and then apply its goodness.

Many Lives, Many Masters is a story about a young woman in her late twenties who is suffering from anxiety, panic attacks, and phobias. Although these symptoms had plagued her since childhood, in the recent past her symptoms had grown worse. She was becoming emotionally paralyzed, unable to cope with reality. Dr. Weiss was recommended to her.

Dr. Weiss was a highly sought-after psychiatrist who at the time of their meeting in 1980 had been appointed chief of psychiatry at a large hospital in Miami, Florida. His credentials are well worth noting. In 1966, he graduated Phi Beta Kappa, magna cum laude from Columbia University in New York. He then went to the Yale University School of Medicine and received his MD degree in 1970. Following an internship at the New York University Bellevue Medical Center, he returned to Yale to complete his residency in psychiatry. Upon completion he accepted a position at the University of Pittsburgh. Two years later, he joined the faculty of the University of Miami, heading the psychopharmacology division. There he achieved national recognition in the fields of biological psychiatry and substance abuse. Four years later he was promoted to the rank of associate professor of psychiatry at the medical school and appointed chief of psychiatry at the university-affiliated hospital previously mentioned.

It would be outlandish for me to attempt to paraphrase his words and thoughts, so I have decided to quote him directly from pages 10, 11, and 12 of his preface to us, his readership.

"Years of disciplined study had trained my mind to think as a scientist and physician, molding me along the narrow paths of conservatism in my profession. I distrusted anything that could not be proved by traditional scientific methods. I was aware of some of the studies in parapsychology that were being conducted at major universities across the country, but they did not hold my attention. It all seemed too farfetched to me."

"Then I met Catherine. For eighteen months I used conventional methods of therapy to help her overcome her symptoms. When nothing seemed to work, I tried hypnosis. In a series of trance states, Catherine recalled past-life memories that proved to be causative factors of her symptoms. She also was able to act as a conduit for information from highly evolved 'spirit entities,' and through them she revealed many of the secrets of life and of death. In just a few short months, her symptoms disappeared, and she resumed her life, happier and more at peace than ever before."

"Nothing in my background had prepared me for this. I was absolutely amazed when these events unfolded."

"I do not have a scientific explanation for what happened. There is far too much about the human mind that is beyond our comprehension. Perhaps, under hypnosis, Catherine was able to focus in on the part of her subconscious mind that stored actual past-life memories, or perhaps she had tapped into what the psychoanalyst Carl Jung termed the collective unconscious, the energy source that surrounds us and contains the memories of the entire human race."

"Scientists are beginning to seek these answers. We, as a society, have much to gain from research into the mysteries of the mind, the soul, the continuation of life after death, and the influence of our past-life experiences on our present behavior. Obviously, the ramifications are limitless, particularly in the fields of medicine, psychiatry, theology, and philosophy."

"However, scientifically rigorous research in this area is in its infancy. Strides are being made to uncover this information, but the process is slow and is met with much resistance by scientists and lay people alike."

"Throughout history, humankind has been resistant to change and to the acceptance of new ideas. Historical lore is replete with examples. When Galileo discovered the moons of Jupiter, the astronomers of that time refused to accept or even to look at these satellites because the existence of these moons conflicted with accepted beliefs. So it is now with psychiatrists and other therapists, who refuse to examine and evaluate the considerable evidence being gathered about survival after bodily death and about past-life memories. Their eyes stay tightly shut."

"This book is my small contribution to the ongoing research in the field of parapsychology, especially the branch dealing with our experiences before birth and after death. Every word that you will be reading is true. I have added nothing, and I have deleted only those parts that were repetitious. I have slightly changed Catherine's identity to ensure confidentiality."

"It took me four years to write about what happened, four years to garner the courage to take the professional risk of revealing this unorthodox information."

"Suddenly one night while I was taking a shower, I felt compelled to put this experience down on paper. I had a strong feeling that the time was right, that I should not withhold the information any longer. The lessons I had learned were meant to be shared with others, not to be kept private. The knowledge had come through Catherine and now had to come through me. I knew that no possible consequence I might face could prove to be as devastating as not sharing the knowledge I had gained about immortality and true meaning of life."

"I rushed out of the shower and sat down at my desk with the stack of audio tapes I had made during my sessions with Catherine. In the wee hours of the morning, I thought of my old Hungarian grandfather who had died while I was still a teenager. Whenever I would tell him that I was afraid to take a risk, he would lovingly encourage me by repeating his favorite English expression: 'vat the hell,' he would say, 'vat the hell.'"

I want to thank Dr. Weiss for his devotion to duty and for having the courage to write his book. I am certain that in 1988 he probably felt if he wrote about his therapy sessions with Catherine he would be putting at risk his entire professional career as a psychiatrist. Perhaps he envisioned losing the respect of his peers or, worse yet, even his practice.

How the book revealed itself to me is still a mystery. Why the book was revealed to me is not. The knowledge I ascertained was so well scripted it erased all the human doubt, guilt, and fear my father had so cleverly and intentionally heaped upon me because of his limited belief systems. It became absolutely crystal clear to me that if what Dr. Weiss discovered was true, then the preconditioned belief systems I grew up with were not wrong, but they were terribly limited in their breadth and scope. If under hypnosis Catherine was able to recant many past lifetimes from ancient to modern day, then the act of reincarnating must be true. If Dr. Weiss is correct and Catherine had the ability under hypnosis to channel information from master spirits, then without a doubt the hierarchy of spirituality is true. I wondered why the message that Jesus the Christ had bestowed upon man had been so watered down. Was it for control or the lack of genuine faith? Christ spoke of developing a faith that is as deep and wide as the oceans, and yet Christ rebuked his disciples for not having as much faith as a tiny mustard seed.

The lesson I learned from reading *Many Lives, Many Masters* is this: I must develop an unquestioning faith and share this information while giving people the freedom to do with this information what they choose to. Human life is an illusion and goes way beyond the five senses.

I realized midway through 2002 that I would not be provided a metaphysical mentor. What I would be provided were uncommon insights that strengthen the mind, the will, and the faith of a man. Beginning in November, 2002, these insights began to emerge. My instincts would be tested time and time again in 2003 and 2004. As Mary predicted, 2002 was a personal challenge.

The Year 2003

As I mentioned in the previous section, my insights began to surface in the month of November, 2002. In that month I warned the supervisors and the partners that the sales in 2003 were going to head south beginning in January of 2003. I explained in great detail that although this was going to happen, if we controlled our costs we could make more profit in 2003 than we did in 2002, but we would have to be steadfast in controlling every line item on our profit-and-loss statements. This was a lofty goal in itself because the twenty-one managing partners had increased sales by $1,342,946 and profit by $673,463 respectively over the previous twelve months that would end in December, 2002.

Again Mary's prediction held true for 2003. It began January 17 when my father had surgery to remove his right leg from the knee down due to poor circulation. Even though my market, as I had predicted, was trending down in sales, I still made several trips to Texas to visit him. I noticed when we were together he was becoming less resistant to spirituality. I knew in my heart his time in this dimension was coming to and end. It was a very difficult situation for me because each time I would see him; his physical body was in decline.

Attempting to find balance in my life by the end of February was becoming a real challenge.

The Merritt convention in 2003 was held at the Hyatt Regency hotel in downtown Albuquerque February 23 through 26. Tuesday night, the twenty-fifth of February, was the night Bobby and Barbie had scheduled the annual masquerade party. Leslie Berryman asked me if I could help a supervisor and his wife who were in trouble with the IRS. I told her I would see what I could do for him. I contacted my accountant and she agreed to meet us for dinner the night of the masquerade party. I never dreamed we would be missed. After all, everyone was in a costume.

About halfway through our meal, I received a phone call from Nick Stamnos, who requested to know my whereabouts. I told him I was at dinner with Cindy and my accountant. He seemed okay with that, but ten minutes later he called me back and very nicely explained to me that Bobby wanted to talk to me immediately. Needless to say, dinner and the meeting were over.

On the way back to the Hyatt, the supervisor admitted he had told his regional director (Bobby's older brother, Tommy) about our meeting with my accountant. He asked to be there when I met with Bobby. I told him that I didn't think that was a very good idea.

Fortunately we were only minutes away from the hotel. As we walked into hotel lobby, Nick was waiting for me. Without a saying a word, he led me around the corner to the lobby bar where Bobby was. I must note that this particular bar is slightly elevated above the lobby's marble flooring. It is also wide open for easy access.

As Nick and I rounded the corner, I spotted Bobby immediately. It was obvious he was not happy. He saw me and abruptly ended his conversation with his brothers and started down the stairs. As far as I could see, the bar was filled to capacity with nothing but SONIC directors, supervisors, managing partners, and their respective spouses.

Bobby timed his descent to the lobby floor to match our arrival. He then led Nick and I approximately fifteen paces away from the bar. Although we were about forty-five feet away, everyone in the bar had first-class seats to the show Bobby was about to put on.

He positioned himself so that for most of the show he and Nick had their backs to the folks in the bar, which of course forced me, as they say, to face the music while I paid the piper.

Our conversation actually started out quite civil. He told me about how much his conventions cost him and that he expected everyone to attend each and every event.

Although he knew the answer to his first question, he asked why I felt it was necessary to take a supervisor, whom I was not even responsible for, out to dinner to meet an accountant. The beginning of my explanation was interrupted with a flurry of innuendos, cuss words, and arm- and hand-waving, followed by a lot of finger-pointing. This abuse went on for so long I honestly lost track of the time.

Never in my lifetime had I ever allowed any man to talk to me in this type of degrading manner—especially when my peers and subordinates were watching and within earshot of what was being said. As Bobby tried to publicly humiliate me, I passively, privately wondered what lesson I was supposed to learn. I could not figure out what I had done that was so terrible. His words were harsh and threatening as he paced around waving his hands and arms, stopping numerous times to shake and point his finger in my face. I was saddened that the leadership of his company had to watch this extravaganza.

As Bobby continued firing off misdirected information, two phrases kept swirling around in my mind: one, "Always praise someone in public and reprimand them in private," and two, "Those who own the gold make the rules." Maybe that was the lesson, learning that Bobby owned all the gold. I could see in his eyes that he wanted to fire me. Instead the butt-chewing ended with Bobby stating emphatically "You have twenty-four hours to decide whether or not you want to be a Merritt!" He then stormed off, leaving Nick and me alone. The only thing I remember Nick saying to me was that he had never seen Bobby so mad.

The next morning I found Bobby in the dining room engaged in a conversation with some of the other SONIC owners who had attended his convention. I didn't want to disturb him, so I waited at the door for him to finish talking. He saw me waiting but he never came over. I finally left.

I found out later that day that Bobby had been drinking pretty heavily the night of the costume party. After hearing that, I wasn't sure whether it was the whiskey talking or if the whiskey had brought out his real feelings toward me.

Either way, it didn't really matter. If I had done what I was getting paid to do, none of this would have ever happened. As a post script, my accountant was able to help the supervisor get out from underneath the IRS. So whatever punishment I received was still worth it. I never called Bobby and he never called me. I just went back to work like nothing had happened.

We opened up another restaurant about a month later. That was the next time I saw Bobby. He apologized the best he could but stood firm that what I had done was unacceptable. That was good enough for me. Sales were trending down as I had anticipated, so I knew it wouldn't be long before Nick and the gang would start asking questions and applying some pressure. What I didn't expect was that Nick was doing a tremendous amount of fishing for information behind my back. Most of the information was personal in nature.

In other words, he was looking for a reason to fire me. I never confronted him about this, because my time and energy was focused on right thinking, right action, right effort, and right understanding. I was putting all my concentration on finding creative ways to ensure my partners and supervisors made more of a profit, because profit directly impacted their income.

Every idea I implemented was scrutinized under the proverbial microscope.

The following are just three examples:

1. We didn't paint the exterior of our buildings, saving the market over 50,000.00 dollars.

Repercussion: sales were down because we looked shoddy.

> We quit taking checks because we had accepted over 40,000 dollars worth of bad checks in 2002. We saved over 37,000 dollars by not taking checks.

Repercussion: sales were down because we offended our guests.

2. Compared to the previous year, we spent 1.3 percent less in labor. Granted, if your sales are down, you will naturally spend less on labor.

Repercussion: sales were down because our service was slow.

Bottom line, by the end of the calendar year, our sales were down just over a million dollars, but our profit was up over 200,000 dollars compared to the previous year, 2002. Also as expected, our customer counts were down 4.3 percent or 146,725 less tickets. Needless to say, that is a huge decline, but it would have affected our store sales even more if I hadn't encouraged our management teams to focus their attention on increasing their average ticket through suggestive selling. I am still convinced this was the reason our average ticket was up four cents on every dollar in sales, without having to increase our menu prices.

As Mary had indicated, I would have many challenges in the year 2003.

The only way to meet these challenges was to trust in my instincts, even though my methodology would not be understood or appreciated. Since I was aware this was going to happen, I just instinctively let the negative comments from my superiors roll off my back.

The last keen insight I want to share with you is my ability to understand the psychological impact that negative sales has on the psyche of all managers, whether they are new to the position or older seasoned veterans. Instead of spending time wisely, logically attempting to figure out why their sales are trending down, managers for some reason instead make up excuses for it through their use of blame.

The first thing they blame is always the weather. "It's been too hot." "It's been too cold." "It's been too windy." "It's been too wet." "It's been too dry." Or "It's been too humid." If sales keep trending down throughout the year, field operators will then shuffle the blame to the marketing department. Now if someone were to ask me if ideal weather patterns or a solid marketing plan would have a positive impact on a fast-food drive-in restaurant concept, my reply would be a definite yes. It would also be yes if the reverse was true. There is no danger in allowing managers some wiggle room to blame sales declines on bad weather or even on their perception of perhaps a poor marketing plan.

Where the danger lies is how upper management handles a down-trending sales decline. If it is handled incorrectly, relationships will deteriorate, affecting the very fabric of operational excellence. If threatened and intimidated, managers will respond the same way to the people they are responsible for. This situation causes turnover, which always increases labor costs and has a negative impact on operations and the individual team members.

So what starts out as a concern for negative sales decline has now spiraled into a three-alarm fire! Individual store morale is poor, labor costs are going up, and upper management didn't fix the unfixable sales trend.

Most likely the store managers would be suffering from "post traumatic stress," worrying so much about their jobs that they would be spending every waking moment trying to cover their mistakes instead of focusing on their store costs and operational excellence.

Reality states that if my market had been down just over a million dollars in sales compared to the previous year, then the profits compared to the previous year should have also been down in the neighborhood of 400,000 dollars.

Why then were the profits up 200,000 dollars when compared to the previous year? Having the faith to believe what I knew in the future would become a reality, my supervisors took the initiative to forewarn the managers of the upcoming sales decline even before it started happening.

My insights and instincts, and my supervisors' patience and fortitude, enabled each of us to take personal risks for the sake of our organization. At the end of the day, although sales were a muck, the morale of the entire Colorado SONIC organization was very high.

I have but one more challenge to share with you before I move into the year 2004. In the early-morning hours of the twenty-second of September, 2003, my father died. My sister and stepmother were with him when he passed quietly at his home in Fort Worth, Texas. At the exact time of his death, I sat up in my bed, wide awake from a very deep sleep. One thought came into my mind: *your dad just died*. As I sat there on the edge of my bed, I thought I heard my father's voice inside my head. "I wanted you to know that I'm okay," he said. I thought I had imagined his voice until he spoke again. "I picked the twenty-second to cross over because I know twenty-two has always been your favorite number." And then I heard him laugh, which caused me to chuckle, knowing he was sitting there beside me in spirit form, letting me know in his own special way I wasn't crazy.

If you have not had the euphoric experience of talking to a spiritual being, it is very much like talking to living human being, except you don't have to move your lips. Their thoughts are able to transcend our human thoughts when they choose to match our vibration pattern, which empowers them to be able to communicate with us.

My father told me that I was on the right path and to disregard the information he had sent to me about cults. He admitted his beliefs had been narrow and he had been too judgmental. He stated he was now aware of the entire truth that extends beyond the human capacity to understand God's beauty and love. He then told me he had been directed to tell me in a very loving way the day, month, and year that I would die. He stated I should write this information down, seal it in an envelope, and file it away in a secure place.

Before I could ask him why this information was being given to me, the phone rang, which ended our conversation. When I picked up the phone, I could hear my stepmother crying. She was calling to tell me my father had just died.

I thanked her for letting me know so soon. I didn't tell her I already knew.

After I had hung up the phone, I curled up in my bed, hoping my father would return, but he didn't. I knew in that moment I was on my own. I thought about what he had said, and then I remembered what Ja-Zon had told me several years before: "Because of your physical and spiritual connection deciding to stay the course no matter what, confirmation of this will occur in the future and be acknowledged in the physical world to you by someone very close to you. You will be told the day, month, and year of your physical departure!"

I immediately got up and went into my office. I wrote down on a piece of paper the date my father had given me. I then put the piece of paper in an envelope, sealed the envelope, and filed it in a secure place. I wrote on the front of the envelope that the envelope was not to be opened until after my death. Why this information needs to be documented and secured is a mystery to me, but I have learned to do what I am told.

You would probably not want to know the exact day you will die, but I, on the other hand, felt relief and a certain amount of comfort. I had always felt since turning thirty that I was on borrowed time. I now knew exactly how much borrowed time I actually have left.

The Year 2004

I discovered quickly in early January that 2004 was going to be a magical, mystifying year. Our food and beverage sales quickly began to recover just as predicted. By June we had recovered all of our losses from 2003.

The Merritt convention for 2003 was celebrated in late February 2004.

The regional directors' responsibilities are to nominate their best candidates for awards based upon their managers' and supervisors' individual performances. The officers of the company always compiled the finally numbers from various sources in order to assist them in determining the winners of those candidates nominated by their directors. Their findings were always closely guarded in secrecy.

For a nominee to win an award, it was mandatory that the nominee have positive sales and customer-count increases by the end of the calendar year. Although I had many managers and supervisors who could have been winners, none of them would be because of the decline in sales and customer counts we had suffered through in 2003. My intention in nominating anyone in my market was the hope they would at least be recognized by standing as their name was mentioned for the awards they were competing for. Under the current format, nobody from Colorado would be allowed to walk up on stage to receive an actual physical award.

The night of the banquet, I received the shock of my life. After a luxurious dinner, Bobby formally announced that the format for winning awards had been changed. The officers had decided to wave the mandatory sales and customer count increase for 2003 because so many deserving managers and supervisors would have been eliminated from the competition.

Needless to say, the Colorado market came home with many of the top awards, including supervisor of the year, won by one of my favorite supervisors, Frank Bravato. Even though I had submitted these folks for awards, none of them expected to win because of the previous format. Besides, our motto in Colorado was *we don't do it for the awards and recognition; we do it for our guests.*

Well to be perfectly honest, it felt really good to stand there in the shadows, watching and applauding so many deserving people from Colorado as they proudly marched up onto the stage to be greeted by Bobby and handed their just rewards. It was a night I will never forget. It was to be the final chapter written in the Colorado Merritt book of records, rewards, and revelations. In June of 2004, Bobby sold us to another franchisee, SONIC Restaurants Incorporated.

I am rarely asleep at the wheel, but this situation caught me totally off guard, blindsiding me like nothing I had ever experienced before. It was for me, personally, a transition I never dreamed would ever happen.

I remember the phone call I received from Bobby early that morning in late June. He requested I reserve a restaurant for the following night that had the facilities to seat the entire market, including spouses. He then requested that I meet with him the morning of the dinner, after which he and I were to meet with all the supervisors. Something really big was on the horizon, but I didn't ask any questions and Bobby didn't offer any explanations.

After our conversation my mind produced a light bulb. I pulled out the old tape recording Mary had made and I listened to part of it again. After finding the location of the information I was looking for, I listened carefully as Mary's words began to resonate inside my head, "In 2004, the company you are working for will attempt to shake up your world. Remain steadfast and respond responsibly, because your work will not be finished." I knew that Bobby was planning on dividing up the company into two sections. Nick Stamnos would be the director of operations for one half of the company, and someone else would be promoted to director of operations for the other half. Maybe Bobby was going to announce that I had been chosen to become the new director of operations. Smiling, I thought to myself that would be enough to shake up anybody's world. All I had to do was remain steadfast and responsible—not a problem for me. I wondered who I would pick to replace me, or would I even have a say so in the selection process? I decided to cross that bridge when I came to it. The only person I shared my vision with was Cindy.

The next morning I awoke with a terrible toothache. The pain was radiating from my neck to the top of my head. This pain was unlike any tooth pain I had ever experienced. It felt like someone was sticking a red hot poker in my upper back molar on the left side. I noticed when I was brushing my teeth that cold water seemed to ease the pain. I quickly went to the kitchen and filled up a glass with ice. As I sucked on the ice chucks, the pain subsided.

I was so pleased because I had to meet Bobby in less than an hour. There wasn't any time to have a dentist check out my tooth.

As I pulled up to the hotel where I was to meet Bobby, I ran out of ice chucks. Thirty seconds later I was in agony. I rushed to the hotel restaurant and found a waitress who produced a glass full of ice for me. As I sucked on the ice, my pain immediately disappeared. I promised her a big tip if she didn't let me run out of ice. She asked me if I needed anything else, and I reiterated to her, "No, just ice please."

Bobby showed up a few minutes later, and I told him about the tooth pain.

He stated ice normally makes a toothache worse. I told him I agreed, but for some reason the ice was masking the pain. Without it, I couldn't have endured the pain.

Ten big glasses of ice later, I wasn't feeling much better. Bobby didn't waste any time explaining to me that he had decided to sell off the Colorado market to SRI. His reasons for doing so made excellent business sense.

Our market was pretty much landlocked, especially in Denver and Colorado Springs, meaning very little future growth. I already knew that. During his negotiations with SONIC Industries, they determined that if he sold off his Colorado holdings to SRI, SI would strengthen his development rights in both his Arizona and Nevada markets. Obviously selling the Colorado market would vastly improve his cash flow, allowing him to develop Arizona and Nevada much quicker.

Bobby stated his biggest fear about selling the market was the people he was leaving behind. He told me he had spent many sleepless nights over the past year worrying about the folks in Colorado. He grinned sheepishly and then smacked his lips. "I think everyone will be very pleased with what I have been able to negotiate with SRI! Every partner will be able to buy 10 to 15 percent more ownership. Your supervisors who are partners will also get to purchase more ownership as well, and your co-managers will be salaried. Co-managers and assistant managers will be provided with benefits. And you, my friend, if you choose to, will be promoted to a full director of operations over all the stores in Colorado, to include the SRI restaurants!"

I laughed to myself about my insight in being promoted to a director of operations. It happened, but not the way I had envisioned it. The thought *steadfast and remain responsible* floated to the surface. I would try my best since my work supposedly was not finished yet.

The supervisors showed up on time, and Bobby patiently answered their concerns, issues, and questions. It was obvious two of them were not happy. I understood their dilemmas. They were free spirits who felt they had been sold into corporate slavery. I knew the managing partners would have similar outlooks. This was not going to be an easy pill to swallow.

After twelve big glasses of ice, I had to excuse myself to use the restroom. While I was in the bathroom, my tooth pain became so intense I thought I was going to pass out. I silently prayed, "Lord, this situation I have to deal with is difficult enough in itself without this tooth pain. Please take this horrible pain away, I ask in Jesus' name, amen!" At that exact moment, the pain was gone and has never returned. I left the bathroom singing softly Amazing Grace. I had just experienced yet another miracle.

After meeting with the supervisors, I got to meet Mike Perry, the senior vice president; Rich Schwabauer, the vice president; and Fran Bordenkircher the regional vice president, to whom I would be directly reporting.

After the informal introductions and small talk, we got right down to business—my personal business, as they say. Mike Perry presented the deal to me, and then after a long pause he asked, "What do you think?"

I looked him straight in the eye and said, "Is that it?"

He was obviously a little uncomfortable. So I asked, "Is this negotiable?"

Now Rich as well as Fran were showing signs of discomfort. Obviously the offer was not negotiable.

So I asked, "Do you really expect me to take a fifty-thousand-dollar-a-year cut in pay?"

Mr. Perry was quick to respond, "Maybe you don't fully understand stock options."

At that time Bobby got up and started to leave. "Where are you going?" I asked.

Bobby chuckled and said, "I've negotiated with you before. You're better off on your own." And then he opened the door and left.

I turned to face Mike once more and said, "I understand your stock options. They're considered future money, if the company does well. But I can't cash them in until after the first year, right?" Mike agreed and then went on to explain how valuable these options become. After he was through, the room fell silent.

Suddenly I remembered what Mary had said: "Remain steadfast and respond responsibly. Your work is not finished yet."

I quickly looked up, surveyed their faces, took a deep breath, and quietly said, "Okay, let's do this deal!" Their smiles lit up the room.

I didn't realize it then, but Bobby told me a few days later his entire deal with SRI and SI hinged on whether I accepted their offer. If I hadn't accepted their offer, I would have blown his deal. I thought perhaps he was exaggerating the situation a bit in order to make me feel a little better—you know, adding a little Bobby Merritt drama—but then he followed his statement up with a comment I had been waiting to hear from him for over eight years. "It takes a whole lot of courage and character to stand by your people in tough situations. Your people need your outstanding leadership, courage, and character to keep it together through this transition period. I know in my heart you have the unique people skills to get this done. I am proud of you."

I told Bobby I appreciated his kind words and that I would remain steadfast and responsible throughout the process.

The next few days were like a West Texas sand storm. Except for a couple of bumps and bruises, the transition went fairly smooth. I was very proud that although many of my folks were brokenhearted, they remained professional in their responses and reactions to the new leadership, their ideas, and the culture they had inherited by osmosis. Within the entire Colorado market, there were only two individual deals that were not substantially better. One, of course, was mine and the other was that of my key supervisor in Denver. Fortunately that supervisor was my eldest son, Kevin Jr. I say fortunately because at least I had some control in assisting him in not only accepting their offer, but privately explaining why his offer was substantially less than what he was currently making.

The offers we were given didn't take into account our income derived from the dividends we received monthly from our ownership interest in two New Mexico SONIC drive-ins that we were partners in. Since we were both now SRI employees, Bobby had to buy out our interests in the two individual restaurants.

The money I received should have been used for investment purposes, but instead some of it had to be used to retire some of my debt. It wasn't that I had been living that far beyond my means; I just enjoyed donating lots of my money to organizations and individuals I knew needed some financial help. It always made me feel good. I know someday I would be in the position to help others again. In addition I often loaned money to people interest-free.

Many times this money was never paid back. That was okay too. It was always my choice and always the right thing to do.

After the smoke had cleared and the SRI teams had gone back to Oklahoma and Bobby's team had gone back to New Mexico, everything slowly got back to being somewhat normal. There were a lot of people who were disconnected and unhappy, but we worked through those issues. I learned patience, understanding, and compassion. I knew everything would be fine.

In finishing off the year 2004, all I can say is the journey was worth it. I have many fond memories to look back on and a basket full of lessons that I learned. SRI turned out to be a wonderful organization with many talented, experienced restaurant experts. The year 2004 turned out to be very exceptional. I want to thank Mike Perry, Rich Schwabauer, and Fran Bordenkircher for having the patience, fortitude, and foresight to help me get over the bumps along the way.

The Year 2005

Fran left the company and was replaced with a newly promoted director from Tulsa, Oklahoma, John Salama. John was a very successful director in the Tulsa market and I expected him to be just as successful as an RVP. He was an honest and a very hard-working man. I had enormous respect for his SONIC knowledge and his powerful network of people within both of the SRI and SI organizations. If I needed something done, he knew exactly who to contact to ensure my needs were met. And I was pretty needy from time to time.

From June of 2004 to August of 2005, we built five SONIC Drive-In restaurants; three in Denver and two in Colorado Springs. That in itself was very demanding. Recruiting, training, and staffing managers were at an all-time high. Additionally I had to promote one manager and two partner/managers to the supervisory rank, which thinned our management depth even more.

Besides opening new stores, it seemed every month Mike Perry had a brand new program he wanted rolled out into the field. The real estate department was made up of movers and shakers too. They kept Rich, John, and I busy looking at new sites. In addition I had to fly to Oklahoma City at least once a month, and on one occasion John had me fly to Tulsa, to spend some quality time in his old market.

When I was in town, most of my time was spent with a young but very aggressive supervisor named Ryan Boothe. It seemed like every time I turned around he wanted to fire some manager. Ryan had enormous talent but very little patience with people. I tried very hard to teach him how to teach, mentor, and coach his people. Thank goodness four of my other supervisors, Greg Wignall, Kevin McPeek Jr., Julie Davidson, and Gordon Pace were taking care of business.

My other supervisor, Frank Bravato, was having a really difficult time adjusting to the culture of SRI. He wasn't sure if he wanted stay or leave. I knew he was talking with other organizations and not spending as much quality time in his restaurants, but I gave him plenty of space in order for him to finally make up his mind. Frank had won the Merritt Supervisor of the Year Award for 2003, and in my opinion that carried a lot of weight. He was terribly disconnected, and if I couldn't find a way to reconnect him, SRI would lose a really valuable player. To make a long story short, it took many months of coaching and listening, but Frank finally reconnected himself.

My biggest issue with the way SRI did business was the amount of e-mails, most of which were duplicates or unnecessary information that was useless out in the field. The directors were still responsible to go through them and reply when necessary to the sender. This squandered a lot of my time that would have been better spend working with my people. My supervisors didn't get near the volume of e-mails I did, but they too found it cumbersome in managing their time.

As I wrote in my preface, by October of 2005 the urge to write was overcoming my ability to focus all my attention on work. It came down to either working or writing. In early November I called John Salama and told him about my dilemma. We had developed a pretty strong bond, and I knew this was going to be hard on him. We discussed it at length and it is my understanding he and Rich discussed it at length too. They were trying to figure out a way that I might be able to write and continue working for SRI.

I knew the demands of the job were too great for this to work out harmoniously. I therefore gave my proper notice and retired the first of January 2006.

And so my journey with SONIC Restaurants came to an end. I will always be grateful for the experiences, the people, the lessons, and the time I spent with both the Merritt family and the SONIC corporate family.

Chapter 22
The Final Chapter

It is now March 1, 2007, fifteen long months since I retired from the restaurant industry. In my wildest dreams I would never have believed it would take me fifteen months to finish this book. What I have discovered in the process is: one, writing a book is a lonely business, and two, it is difficult to turn your thoughts into words, sentences, and paragraphs that accurately convey those thoughts, unless you are inspired to do so.

My hope is that you have not only enjoyed my story, but more importantly you have discovered that in learning to control your thoughts you have the power to create your own world as you choose to. My hope is that you now realize that your thoughts don't have to be on autopilot. If you choose to be happy, peaceful, contented, successful, and compassionate, that's what you will become, no matter what is going on around you. The law of attraction is a combination of your thoughts and feelings. Your actions will always represent your thoughts and feelings.

My hope is that you now understand that you are a spiritual being having a human experience. Developing your faith in the unexplainable will enrich your human life beyond your comprehension. I suggest to you that what you have believed in the past to be coincidental or accidental was actually events and situations created by and through your own personal thoughts. Your human life is a miracle. Learn to make the most of it. My hope is you'll awaken to your truly rich reality and the power that is yours for the taking.

IF you are living in the lower nature, you are naturally living in a state of fear, which makes you feel downtrodden, beat up, mixed up, misunderstood, resentful, disappointed, frustrated, angry, and unhappy. Your thoughts are on autopilot because you have been conditioned to react and respond according to your belief systems that you have put in place in order for you to feel safe and protected. This mangled, entangled web of emotion manifests itself in the form of personal loss, personal persecution, personal hate, personal judgment, personal anxiety, personal stress, and all other negative thoughts. The bottom line is that your suffering stems from belief systems that no longer have to serve you. Wherever you are right now, stop and take one step back and ask yourself why. Why do I feel the way I do? What lesson am I to learn in order for me to move forward? Why am I choosing to live in poverty? Why do I always choose to blame others for my malcontent instead of taking responsibility for my own thoughts and emotions? Why do I see the negative so clearly and the positive so dimly? Why is my life filled with emptiness instead of brimming over with love and gratitude? Why am I addicted to the darker side of life? Simply stated, you are living in your lower nature. Consciously you are not aware that as a physical human being you have the ability to connect to your God self. You are not consciously aware of your blessed dual nature. Instead you continue to allow your ego/personality to expand your personal suffering. This you believe is your true reality. You believe the material world with all of its laws and limitations is your true reality.

My question to you is, why do you feel this way? The answer is, YOU ARE LIVING IN THE FIVE-SENSE WORLD. As I have said before, if you can't see it, if you can't smell it, if you can't hear it, it you can't touch it, and you can't taste it, most of us believe *it* doesn't exist! *It* represents anything that can't be explained scientifically or logically.

I find it very interesting that science, religion, and spirituality appear to be finding some common ground. I find comfort knowing that millions of people are beginning to awaken from a deep sleep to find themselves pondering their purpose.

Our social, cultural, economical, ecological, and medical issues will *never* be resolved until we all understand our dual nature and decide to harness our egos and awaken to our higher nature. It is an amazing journey—one that will dazzle your senses and relax your mind. When you consciously make decisions based on higher-nature thoughts, what you will manifest in the material world will astound, surprise, and delight you.

I dare you to not let people, events, situations, and circumstances affect you in a negative way. I dare you to examine the belief systems that may not be serving you. I dare you to look inside yourself and not outside yourself when faced with conflicts. I dare you to compete within yourself and cooperate outside yourself. I dare you to be the best that you can be.